Broken Alabaster Jars

Faith Writings Volume II
Alisa Hope Wagner

Marked Writers Publishing

Broken Alabaster Jars

Faith Writings Volume II

Broken Alabaster Jars
Faith Writings Volume II
Copyright @ 2015 by Alisa Hope Wagner
Marked Writers Publishing
www.alisahopewagner.com

Scriptures taken from multiple translations of the Bible.

Author photo by Monica Lugo
Edits by Faith Newton

ISBN-13: 978-0692415870
ISBN-10: 0692415874
BISAC: Devotional / Christian / Religious/ Nonfiction

Dedication

God, my Creator, my Savior, my Counselor

Daniel, my high school sweetheart and soul mate

Isaac, my firstborn son

Levi, my brown-eyed boy

Karis Ruth, my cherished girl

Christina, my twin and my friend

Forward

This collection of writings is book 2 of the *Vessels Series* written over a ten-year span. When a life is given over to God's care, a slow transformation begins to take place. It is difficult to explain this change in a bullet list of conclusions. However, the "ever-increasing" transformation can be experienced in real-life stories. That's what this book represents—a glimpse into the heart of an imperfect person in love with a perfect God.

"And we all, who with unveiled faces contemplate the Lord's glory, are being transformed into his image with ever-increasing glory, which comes from the Lord, who is the Spirit" (2 Corinthians 3.18 NIV).

Vessels Series

Imperfect Vessels
Broken Alabaster Jars
Gathering Empty Pitchers

Broken Alabaster Jars

In Mark 14.1-11, Jesus was dining at Simon the Pharisee's house when a sinful woman came and broke an alabaster jar over His body that covered him with a very expensive perfume. The religious leaders were indignant. They shamed her by saying that the money could have been spent on other good works.

I imagine the woman kneeling there. God put a passion in her heart, and she obeyed Him even though she was humiliated in the process. She didn't know that she was anointing the Son of God before His death and resurrection. She just knew that she was being obedient.

She held two broken pieces of alabaster jar in each hand and endured the shame and judgment thrown at her by the religious leaders. They had their agenda of what good works were important, and hers didn't follow suit of what they expected.

Recently, I experienced a time when I began to question the fruit of what God is doing in my life. I wasn't breaking my alabaster jar over a certain good work, and I lost confidence in my God-design and purpose. Were the good work fruits that I was producing a harvest from God? Was I being obedient to His will?

I knelt in my closet holding my pieces of alabaster up to God and

1

begged Him to show me what I was doing wrong. For the past several years, God has completely turned my life upside down. I have been obedient (though, not perfect) to the Holy Spirit's leading. I know that I have changed, but I wasn't directly achieving a specific good-work fruit, and my trust in God and my obedience to Him faltered. Was I really hearing from God?

After I humbled myself before the Lord, God beautifully brought me to a verse about good works. The crowd was searching for Jesus because He just performed many miracles. And they asked Him, "What must we do to do the works that God requires?"

"Jesus answered, 'The work of God is this: to believe in the one he has sent'" (John 6.28-29 NIV).

As I knelt in my closet, God asked me, "Will you believe Me?"

This belief that God requires of me is not just simply a belief that He exists. Many people believe in God and Jesus. This belief He requires of me is a belief that He is creating amazing fruits in my life, and I daily must believe that His promises will come to pass. Good works come in all forms, and they should be an outward expression of my inward relationship with Christ. He doesn't judge my works (my good works will never measure up to God's perfection).

He judges my heart. Do I believe that my simple acts of obedience are valuable to Him even if the world claims them as unimportant? Am I being obedient to His will even though I can't gage or measure the harvest to the world's standard of success?

There are a lot of Christians out there with many passions. This is an awesome thing. We are all called to be the hands and feet of Jesus, and our fruits will all look differently. If you read through Jesus' life in the Gospels, you will see that He harvested many fruits in a vast range of areas.

I believe that we can appreciate every faith-filled good work, but God will give us specific passions for the specific needs He wants us to fill. We are all uniquely designed with a purpose to help in certain areas. We can't all be passionate about the same thing.

My wish is that Christians stop criticizing other Christians for being passionate about different good works. God puts that passion in each of us. We are simply breaking the alabaster jar over our own personal relationship with Christ, and He is directing the flow of perfume, anointing our Kingdom Purposes along the way. The enemy loves it when Christians fight against each other. A house divided will fall. However, as we unite and encourage each other's unique passions, we will become a collective force for good in God's Kingdom.

"Jesus knew their thoughts and said to them, 'Every kingdom divided against itself will be ruined, and every city or household divided against itself will not stand'" (Matthew 12.25 NIV).

3

Citizens of Heaven

I had to be put under for a dental procedure. My single wisdom tooth needed to be pulled, and I can say I was honestly more worried about going under anesthesia than I was having the procedure done. Would I be fully asleep? How would it feel? What really happens as my body slips into unconsciousness?

I laid on the dental bed, surrounded by bright lights and white walls. The dental staff buzzed around me in their normal routine, wearing their little surgical masks. I prayed for them in my slurred speech affected by the laughing gas, and the nurse next to me whispered, "amen."

The real medicine hadn't kicked in yet, and my eyes darted around nervously. The nurse looked at the dentist, and he responded with a quick movement toward my IV. Finally, I felt my body loosen, and my vision quickly tunneled into blackness.

The next thing I remember was my husband walking in and the dentist smiling widely. I couldn't help myself. I thanked the dentist (whose name happened to be Jesus), and I opened my arms wide and gave Jesus a big hug. I was so relieved that the procedure was over, and I was spared the misery of experiencing it!

Sometimes I fear the process of dying. I'm not afraid to die because I know I'll be in heaven with Jesus, but the entire process of losing consciousness and slipping into eternity scares me. What will it feel like? How long will it take? Who will be there when I awake?

I hope that the process will be much like my dental procedure. My earthly eyes will fade to black, and I will awake with Jesus, my Lord and Savior, waiting for me with a wide smile. I will give Him a big hug, and He will say, "Welcome home, my daughter."

"But we are citizens of heaven, where the Lord Jesus Christ lives. And we are eagerly waiting for him to return as our Savior. He will take our weak mortal bodies and change them into glorious bodies like his own, using the same power with which he will bring everything under his control" (Philippians 3.20-21 NLT).

One Talent and Proud

In the Parable of the Talents (Matthew 25.14-27), a master gives money to three of his servants, so they can invest it while he's away. He gives one servant 1 talent, another 2 talents and the other 5 talents. A talent is a measurement (weight) of gold or silver. If the Master was giving gold, the value of one talent would be close to a million dollars today! Needless to say, the master trusted even his 1 talent servant with a great responsibility.

Whenever I read this parable, though, I often times become a little anxious. I wonder if am a 1, 2 or 5 talent kind of girl. Are my "abilities" worthy enough to handle the 5 spot or am I only strong enough for the 1? I know the emphasis of the parable is placed on the effort. No matter what God gives us, we should do our best to invest and multiply it. However, I have trouble with some scholars' opinions that God blesses some people with more talents than others—like somehow there are "Christian Elite," and they have special purposes that surpass the rest of us. The Bible was written for all of us, and the promises that fill it are for each child of God to claim—not just a few.

When I was contemplating all of this, I felt the Holy Spirit tell me that I was looking at the parable one-dimensionally and that there was a fullness that I was missing. Then I realized that I was all three servants. God has blessed me with 1, 2 and 5 talents according to my abilities.

To be honest, I have very few 5 talents, a handful of two talents and a slew of 1-talents. I can comfortably confess that there are many areas where God has given me only 1 talent of ability. I do the best that I can with my 1 talent, but my efforts won't be able to produce what others can produce with their 5 talents.

For example, I find it difficult to speak one-on-one with people. I have friends that take this ability for granted. They don't see what is so special about being able to casually talk about church and life with people they just met. I, on the other hand, am in awe of their communicative suaveness, and I appreciate the amazing gift that they have been given. They have 5 talents in an area that I only have 1. Sometimes, I wish I could just bury my 1 talent in the ground, but God expects me to put forth the effort, even if it's uncomfortable and exhausting for me. Thankfully, though, God usually allows me to rest in this area, and I enjoy taking a backseat to the social butterfly.

When I do run into people face-to-face, I use my 1 talent to the best of my abilities, and I know that God is pleased. I won't ignore people just because I'm uncomfortable. I know that even my 1 talent is worth almost a million dollars, and I won't squander it just because I'm an introvert. Thankfully, God gave me more talents in another form of communication. I love to write. I'm comfortable writing, and I can produce much more at the keyboard than I can at a dinner party. Because I enjoy writing, I don't mind spending time and energy doing it. Sitting at the computer for several hours every night doesn't sound too bad to me (though, that took years of discipline to achieve).

In reality, I wouldn't want to have 5 talents in everything I do. Could you just imagine how draining our lives would be if we were the "bread-winners" in every area of life? When would we ever rest? I love the fact that I don't have to be the one in charge, the one making things happen, the one that everyone looks to or the one that produces the most all of the time. I value that God chose to give me a break when He designed me with many 1-talent abilities. I might have a lot to say at the keyboard; but if you find me at a dinner party, I'll be the one in her seat, enjoying the ability to just sit and listen. Sure, I'll talk if

God urges me to, but normally He allows me to be a fly on the wall.

"In his grace, God has given us different gifts for doing certain things well. So if God has given you the ability to prophesy, speak out with as much faith as God has given you. If your gift is serving others, serve them well. If you are a teacher, teach well. If your gift is to encourage others, be encouraging. If it is giving, give generously. If God has given you leadership ability, take the responsibility seriously. And if you have a gift for showing kindness to others, do it gladly" (Romans 12.6-8 NLT).

Rushing Truth

The college years should also be known as the broke years. I waitressed and attended classes full time, and money always seemed to be a scarce commodity in my life. One semester, I took a black and white photography class. Little did I know how much photography equipment cost!

I used every dime I had to purchase the materials that I needed.

During class, my photography professor announced that she would be holding a workshop for those of us who wanted additional instruction. The cost of the workshop would be $12. I opened my wallet and noticed that I had exactly $12 to my name. Of course, I would have to skip lunch for a few days and beg some rice and beans from my restaurant manager before work, but it would be worth it!

Although the money wasn't due for another month, I decided to pay her the cash early. My professor hurriedly took my money without writing my name down and said she needed to run off to lunch. A few days later, I discovered that I had a conflicting engagement and I would not be able to make the workshop. Before the next class, I explained to the professor that I wouldn't be able to attend. She looked at me confused. Then I asked if she wouldn't mind refunding my money.

Sadly, she had been so rushed during our exchange the previous day that she completely forgot that I had signed up and given her money. Since she wrote nothing down, there was no proof. Even if I had wanted to attend, there was no record that I had paid the fee!

I tried to recharge her memory.

I described how she had been rushing out to lunch when I gave her the $12, and that she had put the money in her wallet. But she insisted that our exchange never happened. What could I do? My $12 seemed like a fortune to me, but I couldn't emphasize a memory to my professor that she obviously didn't care to keep.

This incident taught me a valuable lesson. I always want to give people the benefit of the doubt. I don't want to be so self-assured in how I see things that I'm unable to hear others out, especially those who look up to me. I can wisely decipher whether I'm speaking a truth of the Holy Spirit or if my own pride is demanding to be right.

No matter what, I can still receive and respect the opinions of others. I realize that I will never be perfect, so I can partner my opinion with five valuable words: "…but I may be wrong."

Humility will always lead to honor, so there is no need to prove myself (Proverbs 18.12). The truth will come out eventually, and I never want to lose my integrity over *$12*.

"For there is nothing hidden that will not be disclosed, and nothing concealed that will not be known or brought out into the open" (Luke 8.17 NIV).

New Creation

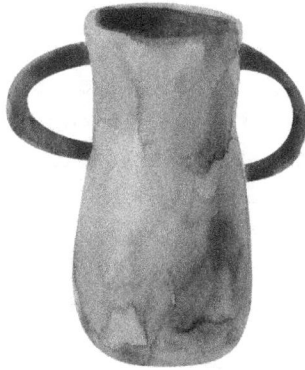

Every year before the holiday rush, I try to be very intentional about maintaining an atmosphere of peace and joy in my life. When I was younger, I used to allow the busy schedule of cultural expectations to actually prevent me from enjoying the most celebrated season of all—Jesus' birthday! Now, I take the time to ask myself one important question: "Am I experiencing joy?"

You see, when the angels went to the shepherds to declare the birth of Jesus, they said specifically that His birth would cause "great joy" to all people!

"But the angel said to them, 'Do not be afraid. I bring you good news that will cause great joy for all the people'" (Luke 2.10 NIV).

So if I'm not experiencing the joy of Christ, it's not because Jesus didn't do His job. We can know for sure that Jesus atoned for the sins of the world because we have the presence of the Holy Spirit. The Holy Spirit finding residence in our hearts is proof that Jesus' finished work on the cross was successful!

Therefore, if there is a lack of joy in my life, the problem is hidden somewhere in me. What is robbing the fullness of my joy this year? What can I change in my thinking to allow the joy of the Lord to permeate my heart? Has any corrupted belief system stolen the joy that is rightfully mine in Christ?

This year I examined my heart and identified what was stealing some joy in my life. The Bible says that we become a "new creation" in Christ. And I realized that I wasn't fully embracing the person who God designed me to be. I wasn't being purposeful about discovering who I am in Christ and finding joy in His wonderful design.

Sometimes I think I focus on how God created everyone else, and I neglect the person that I'm becoming in Him. It is not selfish to want to know who we are in Christ. In fact, it would be hard to accomplish all the great things God has for us if we don't know ourselves. I not only want to know who I am, but I want to find joy in it!

I choose to be excited about the simple attributes of my personality and the unique qualities of my life, so that the joy of the Lord will always be apparent in my words and actions. I am determined to find peace in how God created me, so I can rejoice the birth of my Savior with my one-of-a-kind shout of joy!

"I praise you because I am fearfully and wonderfully made; your works are wonderful, I know that full well" (Psalm 139.14 NIV).

Numbered Days

"Teach us to number our days, that we may gain a heart of wisdom" (Psalm 90.12 NIV).

I love celebrating the New Year. As each year flips to the next on our calendars, we learn to "number our days." Life on this earth allows us to become the people we will be for eternity. We have many chances in the life we've been given, but we only have one life to mature spiritually into our heavenly existence.

Sometimes we can get so caught up in daily living that we forget to have an eternal perspective. But when we have our eyes on heaven and our feet on the ground, we can live as Jesus lived. He balanced the natural and supernatural worlds perfectly. He kept His focus on the Father, allowing the circumstances and people surrounding Him to be caught up in His eternal view.

The key to Jesus' success is prayer. A prayer life provides God an open platform to sit with us, face to face. Prayer is not just an action; it's a state of being. As God allows our public ministry for Him to expand, our private ministry with Him must grow as well.

When we compare our public ministry to a mountain, our private ministry can be compared to a valley. The bigger the mountain, the bigger the valley must be to contain it. Our influence for God should directly parallel our intimacy with Him. Only through abiding with God in prayer and Bible reading will we keep our focus on heaven as we serve God on earth.

When we number our days, we realize that we don't have time to waste not sitting with God in prayer. Only He knows our purpose. Only He knows His Kingdom Plan. He will reveal small steps along the way, but we must sit in His presence to gain His direction, strength and provision each day. So this year, let us resolve to pray, so we can mature in faith and accomplish our God-given destinies!

"But Jesus often withdrew to lonely places and prayed" (Luke 5.16 NIV).

The Unwise Tooth

I was talking to a tech guy at a computer store and somehow we got to chatting about my church. I explained to him that I loved my church, and I invited him to attend if he didn't already have a church home. He was gracious and explained that although he was a Christian, for personal reasons, he chose not to attend church.

I desired to explain to him how much the church aspect of the Body of Christ has strengthened and transformed my faith, but no matter how I tried to explain my thoughts, I always came out sounding "religious." But how could I explain to this man that it's not about checking the "church box" on our to-do list. It's about encouraging and admonishing fellow sojourners in this temporal world and living out our faith together. God's Church is not perfect, but He surely is, and He moves mightily through a throng of people who are pressing toward one goal: daily leading people closer to Christ.

Several weeks later, I was driving home from the dentist. It seems that my one and only wisdom tooth has not stopped growing. In fact, it is much longer than the other teeth in my mouth. The dentist explained that since the tooth has no abutting tooth, there is nothing to halt its growth. My one "unwise" tooth has grown so long that it has been chewing into my bottom gum. I have this beautiful tooth that is completely useless. Moreover, it has become a nuisance to the rest of my mouth and needs to be pulled out!

I fear that's what can happen to Christians who choose not to attend church. We are all seemingly holy and perfect when we are alone, but put us around people, and we'll blow it every time. It is the Body of Christ that develops our faith and protects us from our own inner growth of selfishness, and the Church is the Crown Jewel of this Body. Churches will never perfect, but they each are given a special revelation of God's Kingdom. As long as Jesus and salvation through the cross play center stage, the Church can be a powerful force of God. We need to be a part of this force.

The more we unite, the stronger we will be for Jesus!

"Although I hope to come to you soon, I am writing you these instructions so that, if I am delayed, you will know how people ought to conduct themselves in God's household, which is the church of the living God, the pillar and foundation of the truth" (1 Timothy 3.14-15 NIV).

A Necessary Hedge

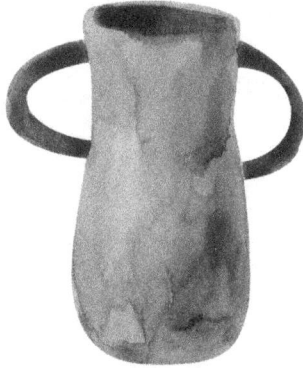

Christians like to pray a "hedge of protection" around themselves and the ones they love. However, many times it is this "hedge" that we are protesting. God will take us on a journey that exposes our inadequacies and inabilities and reveals our need for Him. He allows us to wrestle with Him until we finally die to self and arise in the likeness of Christ.

During this struggle, God will grow this "hedge" high around us, limiting our sphere of influence. He isolates us and does a work in our inner person, perfecting and refining us. We complain because we feel alone, and we think that God is preventing us from fulfilling the great purposes He has created for us.

But He is not limiting us. He is breaking us, and the enemy does not want any person to be broken before God. Satan knows that a humble, meek spirit is a mighty force in God's powerful hands. God creates a "hedge," so the beautiful process of breaking is not interrupted or thwarted.

It is interesting that the process of breaking in our own personal hedge seems inconvenient and even a waste of time to this temporal world, but it is a magnificently essential process in the eyes of eternity. Our brokenness allows the light of God to shine through our lives and nothing could be more breathtaking than a person surrendered to God's glory.

"The high and lofty one who lives in eternity, the Holy One, says this: 'I live in the high and holy place with those whose spirits are contrite and humble. I restore the crushed spirit of the humble and revive the courage of those with repentant hearts'" (Isaiah 57.15 NLT).

In the Rawness

In the waiting, God is able expose our need for Him. He strips us of all worldly good until there is nothing left, and then He affirms His love for us in our rawness. Deep in the middle of who we are—struggles, flaws and weaknesses—God sees in us the image of Himself through the lens of Jesus Christ.

It is at this point of exposed vulnerability that we no longer rely on our own strength. God lights our darkness—not to shame us but to teach us to lean solely on Him. Basing our worth on anything other than Jesus' eternal work on the cross is an injustice to our own soul. Nothing has value outside of our relationship with God through Jesus.

Once God snuffs the lights of our self-efforts, He electrifies our lives with the brilliance of His glory. With hands outstretched, we receive the intensity of our Creator God and wonder why we sought the dim glints of human ingenuity. Surrender is the only path to supernatural living. Humility is the only source of eternal honor.

Humans fester under the heat of self-glory, but under the shadow of God's glory, we flourish and fly. Let us throw the tiny torches of our self-proclamation to the winds and run to the all-consuming fire of Christ in and around us. Let us not ask for God to provide, but let us recognize that God is our provision. He is our hope. He is our purpose. He is our promise.

Let us begin each day by clinging to Christ, knowing that our work will be an overflow of His Indwelling Spirit within us.

"Who among you fears the Lord and obeys the word of his servant? Let the one who walks in the dark, who has no light, trust in the name of the Lord and rely on their God. But now, all you who light fires and provide yourselves with flaming torches, go, walk in the light of your fires and of the torches you have set ablaze. This is what you shall receive from my hand: You will lie down in torment" (Isaiah 50.10-11 NIV).

Working It Out

When I had to buy a new step for the step aerobics I do at home, I noticed there was a new product at the sport's store: a slanted step. I wondered how the slanted step differed from the flat one, so I figured I would buy it and see.

I had a difficult time getting used to the slant. I constantly looked down at my feet to ensure I wasn't about to fall off. And I was more careful doing the aerobic moves that used to be so easy for me. I felt like I was balancing more, and the full length of my foot never seemed to touch the step. I was always on the balls of my feet!

Afterwards, I was exhausted and sweaty, so I knew the work out was a success. However, little did I know just how sore my calves would be the next day—and the following several days thereafter! I could barely walk the next morning. A small touch or rub to my calves caused me to yelp in pain. I've done step aerobics all my adult life and never had I been so sore!

The worse part was that I had a writing deadline, so I didn't work out for the next three days. I kept hoping each morning that my calves would feel less tense, but they became stiffer. As I sat on the computer for hours a day, I knew my stagnant leg muscles were getting clogged with lactic acid.

I needed to get up and work them out! Finally, on the fourth day after my slanted step adventure, I got on my treadmill and ran. Each step hurt at first; but after a while, the tension building up finally began to release. The next morning my calf muscles felt so much better.

This story reminds me that when we are emotional or spiritually tense, sore or upset, the last thing we need to do is fall into a stagnating hole of depression and self-pity. We need to get up and run to God!

We can wrestle through our faith with God, and He will help make our spiritual and emotional muscles stronger. Yes, the process hurts a little bit. Yes, the first steps are the hardest to take. But we can't let the acid of the enemy build up in our lives, causing damage to our hearts and minds. Freedom and joy await us at the end of our struggle if we are willing to work through the pain with God and His Spirit!

"Therefore, my beloved, as you have always obeyed, not as in my presence only, but now much more in my absence, work out your own salvation with fear and trembling; for it is God who works in you both to will and to do for His good pleasure" (Philippians 2.12-13 NKJV).

Stuck in God's Word

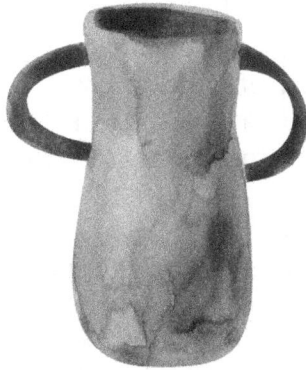

My personal Bible reading time consists of reading through the Bible—Old Testament and New Testament—over and over again. Once I hit the end of Revelation, I head back up to the beginning of Genesis for another read. Last week, I found myself thick in the laws of Leviticus.

"Oh," I thought. "Do I really have to read all these laws again? Can't I just skip them? Is God really going to show me something new?"

I recall that I couldn't get past chapter five of Leviticus. Every morning I'd wake up and reread it. The entire week was rushed for me because I still hadn't adjusted to daylight saving, so I would fly through my quiet time frustrated that I woke up so late.

Each time I read chapter five, I would come up empty: no revelation, no encouragement, no growth. But somehow I found myself looking at the same verses every morning.

Finally, one evening I realized that several days had passed since I had truly heard from God, and I was determined to give Him my full attention. I could tell through my irritable actions of the day that I was not being spiritually fed. In fact, I was starving for God's Truth!

I grabbed my Bible and several other resources and headed to a room on the opposite side of the house. I would not let anything, especially technology, distract me from hearing from the Lord!

Again, I read chapter five of Leviticus, knowing and believing that God had something to tell me or I wouldn't be there still. And there I found it—a jewel hidden deep in God's Word just for me to claim! The revelation hurt my pride a little bit, but I devoured the insight that would ultimately give me peace and joy through a spirit of humility.

"Thank You, Lord, for not giving up on me. Thank You for causing me to be stuck in Your Word, so I could claim your Revelation!"

"Indeed, if you call out for insight and cry aloud for understanding, and if you look for it as for silver and search for it as for hidden treasure, then you will understand the fear of the Lord and find the knowledge of God" (Proverbs 2.3-5 NIV).

Prisoner of Hope

"Return to your stronghold, O Prisoners of hope; today I declare that I will restore you double" (Zechariah 9.12 ESV).

Hope emanates easily when glimmers of it glisten over the shadows of our darkest situations. However, when the lights around us diminish and all the good in this life seem to disappear, hope hurts with an impatient ache.

Hope halts the closure of disappointment and forces us to linger in faithful waiting. It holds onto an allusive promise hidden somewhere in the impossible, and we must remain—exposed and vulnerable—tethered to the tender chains of expectation.

God has entrapped us in His promise and has allowed the promise to perish. And He patiently wills us to endure our devastation, knowing full well that He can supernaturally resurrect the dead into a double blessing. Our wait awakens a heart revolution if we endure hope's season of winter.

But will we sojourn with hope? Will we stay imprisoned in her arms and allow her to nourish the fragile roots of our faith? To be certain, hope will press hard on our soul, causing the breath of our yearnings to wane. Shall we exhale our entitlements and learn to inhale anew, breathing in the rich oxygen of His Life, His Truth and His Way?

We gasp for air and call for our Father to liberate us from hope's fierce embrace. Yet, He tarries for the moment, allowing hope's transforming work to change us. The brilliant glow of hope no longer illuminates the world around us, for she has penetrated deep within, transforming our personal night into glory.

Finally, hope throws open the prison doors, and we dance from our sentence of despair into the radiance of faith displayed (Hebrew 11.1). Our hope renews our strength and vigor; and we realize that the dazzling light dispersing the darkness is shooting through us like the sun. Then we can boldly claim our prize, the double blessing—a promise fulfilled and a life eternally altered (Proverbs 13.12).

"But those who hope in the LORD will renew their strength. They will soar on wings like eagles; they will run and not grow weary, they will walk and not be faint" (Isaiah 40.31 NIV).

The Missing Texts

Almost a week had gone by, and I still hadn't received reply texts from several of my friends. I sent one friend a silly photo. I asked another a question. And I was trying to make arrangements with the other friend. Yet, none of them replied back. I struggled with not being offended by this compound shunning.

I had to capture every negative thought. I knew my friends, and they almost always communicate back with me in a day or two when they get a chance. However, it had been six days and I began to worry. Did I do something wrong? Were they busy? Did I somehow offend them? And I wrestled with anxious thoughts that I knew were wrong.

As I tried to find reasons for their lack of communication, I felt the Holy Spirit say, "Does it matter?" I realized that as a Christian I'm called to love with a love that overlooks all wrong. My focus should be so much on Jesus that my initial knee-jerk reaction in every situation is made in love, truth and forgiveness.

Finally, after I found peace in my circumstances, I discovered that I hadn't been getting any of my text since I bought my new phone six days before. My friends hadn't been ignoring me. I had been ignoring them! Thank goodness they saw the best in me and overlooked my lack of communication!

"Hatred stirs up conflict, but love covers over all wrongs" (Proverbs 10.12 NIV).

Faith in Despair

"Look, God is greater than we can understand. His years cannot be counted" (Job 36.26 NLT).

Job and Elihu finally have their face-off before the throne of God. Elihu is young, vigorous and filled with the understanding of God's faithfulness. Elihu's name means, "My God is YAWEH," in Ancient Hebrew.

Job on the other hand is older, weary and filled with doubt and confusion about God's faithfulness. Job's name means, "Persecuted and hated," in Ancient Hebrew.

Both these men represent a collision point in every Christian's life. There will come a time in our lives where we must choose to cling onto God's faithfulness even when the bottom drops out of our world.

It is easy to claim faith when our health, finances, relationships and ministries are going well. But the real test is whether we cling onto His faithfulness when the trappings of this world persecute us with blows of mistreatment and lack.

Will we remain faithful to God even when the presence of all His good is hidden from us? Will we be shaken by our situation or remain rooted to the truth that "God is greater than we can understand"?

When our experience tells us the situation is hopeless, our steadfastness becomes worn-out and our lives are persecuted to the point of hatred, we can stand on the understanding that God's faithfulness does not change with our circumstance! He is the same yesterday, today and forever; and His faithfulness never ends (Hebrews 13.8).

In the middle of Job's despair, we must claim Elihu's spirit of faith!

Every person struggles with maintaining Elihu's faith when the season of difficulty seems as hopeless as Job's time of hardship. However, we must look past our troubles to a God who is mighty to save (Zephaniah 3.17)! And just like Job, we can trust that though the pain may last the night, joy will come in the morning (Psalm 30.5).

"Instead of your shame you will receive a double portion, and instead of disgrace you will rejoice in your inheritance. And so you will inherit a double portion in your land, and everlasting joy will be yours" (Isaiah 61.7 NIV).

Forsaken Weakness

"But he said to me, 'My grace is sufficient for you, for my power is made perfect in weakness.' Therefore I will boast all the more gladly about my weaknesses, so that Christ's power may rest on me" (2 Corinthians 12.9 NIV).

Lately, I've been thinking a lot about my weaknesses. One of my biggest struggles is insecurity. A long time ago, the Holy Spirit showed me that my insecurity is rooted in pride. I can't be perfect; therefore, I'm insecure. Pride is a sticky sin that sinks beneath the seams, masquerading as something reasonable, as it slowly poisons our souls.

I guess that's where God's grace and my humility collide. I must learn to walk in His strength even with my obvious flaws marking up my life. I must choose to walk in confidence of what Jesus did on the cross and not allow my meager accomplishments to mask my worthlessness without Christ.

But I've also been thinking about God's power. Paul states in 2 Corinthians that God's power is made perfect in my weakness. After wrestling with my weakness for many years, releasing it to God and trying to prevent it from tainting my vision, I think I've finally figured out how God's power is made perfect in this weakness of mine.

It forces me to forsake myself.

I know with certainty that my weakness mucks up my perspective. My insecurity tempts me to seek self-glory, look for flaws in others, question my faith and doubt my abilities in Christ. My weakness robs me of peace, sapping my joy and diminishing my hope, and it fills me with rampant thoughts of worry and despair. I can't trust myself with this weakness, so I have to rely entirely on God.

I die to self, so I can finally have life in Christ (Galatians 2.20). My weakness causes me to be so dead to self that I can boast in that weakness because it causes me to cling to Christ! It's not my strengths, talents or abilities that cause me to forsake self; it's my weakness. And once I've learned to walk outside of my natural tendencies and live fully in the Spirit, God will restore my soul and lead me along paths of righteousness (Psalm 23.2-3).

I abandon my weakness for the perfection of Christ that is mine by faith! Once I've surrendered that weakness to God, the power of Christ will have full reign to shine through.

Choice Words

My parents and aunt came down for a visit; and after four days of nonstop talking, my voice slowly disappeared as each of my confident utterances rang out.

Having an overused voice makes one seriously ponder her choice of words.

My voice is a limited commodity, and I desire to use my words with purpose. However, as my throat restricted in exhaustion, I was left with a weary feeling that I wasted my energy on empty words. Once I waved goodbye to my family, I had a sneaking suspicion that I gave more verbal fortitude to my limited perspective than to God's boundless understanding.

Did my words add value to others? Were my opinions eternally minded? Was my voice used to speak life or death?

Sadly, being around people with whom I was comfortable gave my tongue liberty to speak thoughts that were not bridled to the Holy Spirit. I gave my two cents as I saw things; and in retrospect, I wasted my voice on words that did not speak love, mercy and grace.

And that's when God gave me the Scripture: "A truly wise person uses few words…" OUCH!

I can honestly say that of all of the people sitting around my table, partaking in the family's conversation until the late hours of the night, I was definitely not the wisest. But I have confessed my sin, and I have asked the Holy Spirit to guard my words.

Hopefully, next time my voice will be used to speak life, and I won't waste my energy on petty opinions that don't matter.

I'm determined to allow God to teach me how to use my words according to His desired purpose for His Kingdom on this earth.

I choose choice words.

"A truly wise person uses few words; a person with understanding is even-tempered" (Proverbs 17.27 NLT).

Eternal Partner

When I was about seven years old, my mom brought me and my twin sister to an overnight camp. We were so excited! We had never been camping outside all night long, and I couldn't wait for this new adventure. We'd be away from our parents for 24 hours, and we would meet new people, play new games and explore new territory!

My mother walked my sister and I to the registration and gave the woman at the table my name. My mom handed me my sleeping bag and backpack and gave me a kiss and a hug. Then, she told me that my twin wouldn't be staying at the camp. My mom explained that she was taking my sister home to spend some much needed time with her.

What? I couldn't believe it. I had never once in my life been without my twin sister for 24 hours. Immediately, my demeanor changed. The adventure was no longer camping; it was now being without my twin. I didn't know how to act. I didn't say a word to anyone. I felt like everything was strange, and I was seeing life through brand-new eyes. Even at such a young age, I felt unsure and insecure in this new experience without my twin.

Luckily, as Christians, we never have to be alone. Once we accept Jesus as our Lord and Savior, we receive the Holy Spirit into our hearts and lives. The Holy Spirit stays with us every moment of every day. We must not take His presence for granted because He is the Spirit of God. He is all-knowing, all-peace, all-joy, all-love, all-confidence, all-power; and He has all the resources of the universe at His disposal.

We can go into every new adventure with bold confidence because we know that the Holy Spirit is with us! He will guide us, comfort us and protect our way along righteous paths (Psalm 23.2). The Holy Spirit is our Eternal Partner. God wanted to be with us so much that He sacrificed Himself in the form of Jesus in order to walk with us even in our sinful state. The Holy Spirit's presence in our lives was bought at the cross!

So let's begin to get to know this Holy Spirit inside of us. Let's lean on His understanding. Let's ask Him what He thinks about our situations. Let's discover His will for our lives. Let's get to know the exciting purposes He has planned for us before time began (Jeremiah 29.11). Let's communicate with the Holy Spirit and grow so completely in love with His presence that we feel uncomfortable doing anything without His involvement!

"I still have many things to say to you, but you cannot bear them now. When the Spirit of truth comes, he will guide you into all the truth, for he will not speak on his own authority, but whatever he hears he will speak, and he will declare to you the things that are to come. He will glorify me, for he will take what is mine and declare it to you. All that the Father has is mine; therefore I said that he will take what is mine and declare it to you" (John 16.12-15 ESV).

The Power of Ask

Sometimes we have to make an "ASK" of ourselves. From personal experience, this is one of the most difficult things to do. It exposes our need and humbles our pride.

However, I do believe that many people take asking way too far. They either come at others with an atmosphere of entitlement or they forget that God is their ultimate provider. They knock on everyone's door for help except for our God who makes all things possible according to His Kingdom (Matthew 19.26).

With that being said, I know that from the Scripture, God continually leads people into situations where they have to make an "ASK" of themselves.

Joseph asks Pharaoh's chief cupbearer to remember him when he is restored to his position (Genesis 40.14). Moses asks for provisions from the people to build the Tabernacle (Exodus 25.2). David asks for food for himself from Ahimelech the priest (1 Samuel 21.3) and food for his soldiers from the rich man Nabal (1 Samuel 25.6-8). Elijah asks a destitute widow for a jar of water and some bread (1 Kings 17.11). Paul asks for donations for the Church of Jerusalem (1 Corinthians 16.1-4). And Jesus asks the Samaritan woman for a drink of water from the well (John 4.7).

God loves relationships, and He has formed us into a single unit (the Body of Christ), so we can serve others while also receiving help. Our "ASKS" will always be a part of God's movement in our lives. I enjoy the story in Genesis of how Isaac obtains his bride, Rebekah. Through the setting, characters and plot of this beautiful drama, God shows us something truly powerful about the "ASK."

Abraham asks his servant to find his son, Isaac, a wife from among his relatives. Therefore, the promise of future generations (Isaac) needs a wife (the platform for which the promise can manifest). The servant goes to the city of Nahor and prays to God to help make his matchmaking endeavor a success (Genesis 24.1-66).

Rebekah (who is the symbolic Platform) for Isaac (who is the symbolic Promise) arrives at the well, which is symbolic of God's divine abundance. The setting is in place. We have all the counterparts ready. God has arranged all the players: God's abundance, the Platform and the servant (symbolic of the Holy Spirit) who is working on behalf of the Promise. But everything hinges on one little thing: an ASK!

"Then the servant ran to meet her [Rebekah] and said, 'Please give me a little water to drink from your jar'" (Genesis 24.17 ESV).

Because of the servant's "ASK," Rebekah sees the need and makes a choice to fill it (she offers water to the servant and the camels). And her service to the servant ignites amazing blessings in her own life— she pretty much becomes rich, influential and adored overnight.

Although our continued prayers, petitions and requests must be offered to God, the Supreme Giver, the Holy Spirit will move us to make and "ASK" of ourselves to others.

I think maybe our "ASK" shows our humanity (we are creatures that receive everything) and our humility (we willingly let go of our pride to show our need for something greater than ourselves). And this little "ASK" directed and prepared by the Holy Spirit allows the wellspring of God's abundance to pour forth in our lives. So we can make an "ASK" of ourselves, knowing that God has placed our blessing on the other side of our humility.

"Whatever you ask in my name, this I will do, that the Father may be glorified in the Son. If you ask me anything in my name, I will do it" (John 14.13-14 ESV).

Fight the Good Fight

Once we receive salvation, God promises us peace. We will have peace knowing that we will spend eternity with God (John 10.29), peace knowing that we have purpose in Christ (Ephesians 1.11), peace knowing that we are loved and valued by God (Romans 5.8); however, when we receive Christ as our Lord and Savior, the "work" of salvation has just begun.

Paul exhorts us:

"So then, my dear ones, just as you have always obeyed [my instructions with enthusiasm], not only in my presence, but now much more in my absence, continue to work out your salvation [that is, cultivate it, bring it to full effect, actively pursue spiritual maturity] with awe-inspired fear and trembling [using serious caution and critical self-evaluation to avoid anything that might offend God or discredit the name of Christ]" (Philippians 2.12 AMP).

This struggle or "working out" of our salvation continues on this earth because we will always have our flesh battling our God-breathed spirit. Paul also says in Romans, "I do not understand what I do. For what I want to do I do not do, but what I hate I do" (7.15 NIV).

When we lay our soul on the table and allow God to dissect our inner being, He will expose the default setting of selfishness in our human nature. And once we see our pride and sin spread out before us, we must make a conscious choice every day to walk outside of our flesh and in the spirit.

"I say then: Walk in the Spirit, and you shall not fulfill the lust of the flesh" (Galatians 5.16 NKJV).

We choose every day to walk in the spirit, believing, claiming and living out the truth that we are the righteousness of God through Jesus Christ: "For our sake he made him to be sin who knew no sin, so that in him we might become the righteousness of God" (2 Corinthians 5.21 ESV).

Those who are not struggling in their salvation are those who are blindly and resolutely walking in the middle of their pride, criticism, judgment, bitterness, selfishness and sin unabated and untested. They have no struggle because they have not allowed themselves to stand naked before an all-knowing God.

To be sure, God knows the deepest, darkest spots in all of us; but if we hide behind the fig leaves of our minds (Genesis 3.7), we will never allow ourselves to become accountable. Our pride will become the blanket sin that causes us to never grow from glory to glory in Christ (2 Corinthians 3.18). Pride deceives us and keeps us from God's best and His greater glory (Jeremiah 49.16).

If you are struggling to work out your salvation, be encouraged! You are fighting the good fight of faith!

"Fight the good fight of the faith. Take hold of the eternal life to which you were called when you made your good confession in the presence of many witnesses" (1 Timothy 6.12 NIV).

A Sling and God

Often times we expect God to bring our promises into fruition using the most extraordinary resources and in the trendiest of ways. But our eyes are stuck in the culture of our world, and we forget that Jesus' trade as a carpenter and His obedience to die a sinner's death disappointed and confused even his closest of friends.

When David fought Goliath, God did not give him Saul's sword (1 Samuel 17.39) or an iron spear like Goliath's (1 Samuel 17.7). David took the lowliest of weapons, a sling, and found rocks on the ground. David knew that the battle would not be won by manmade devices because only God would claim the victory. David overcame his enemy with a child's toy and the mighty hand of God.

God uses the mundane and trivial to confound the world (1 Corinthians 1.27). He can turn an old man into a father of nations (Abraham), a jailbird into a prime minister (Joseph), a shepherd into a king (David), a farmer into a prophet (Elisha), a fisherman into a church leader (Peter) and a murderer into an apostle (Paul). God does not need the wonders of this world to fulfill His purposes because He alone is the author of wonder.

Don't run away from the lowly. God will use your normal to claim His victory. Closeness to God is all you need to walk in His promises.

Forget about the swords of all the King Sauls and the spears of all the Goliaths of this world. Cling to your sling, pick up what is around you and give it all you've got! God will shine His glory in your belief alone.

"So David triumphed over the Philistine with a sling and a stone; without a sword in his hand he struck down the Philistine and killed him" (1 Samuel 17.50 NIV).

Light's Aquarium

In the house where I grew up, there were large skinny windows on either side of the front door. These windows allowed sunlight to shoot into the house like laser beams. One of these laser beams landed directly in the middle of the staircase that was located in front of the door.

I used to sit on a wooden step and allow the heat and light of the sunbeam to shine around me. I waved my hands through the sunbeam and exposed different parts of my skin—face, arms, legs, neck—to its light. I would stretch up on my toes and reach my hands up to the ceiling so I could drown my entire body in its warmth.

Needless to say, I could sit and play with my sunbeam for quite a while. However, one particularly bright afternoon, I noticed something. I could see little things floating around in my sunbeam. It looked like a tiny ocean of living creatures dancing and swimming in the light. I couldn't believe it. I looked all around the sunbeam for more floaty-things but couldn't see any. They only existed in the sunbeam's light.

I sat staring at the beam trying to understand why I had never been told about tiny little life forms (particles in the air) floating in the rays of the sun when I realized that the life-forms were actually everywhere—the sunbeam had just illuminated them. My face scrunched up with disgust as I took another breath—I was breathing in little floaty-things!

After a few breaths, I decided that I wasn't going to die and that the little life forms wouldn't hurt me. Although I didn't like seeing the floaty-things, I continued to visit my sunbeam because it was too special for me to let go. This sunbeam reminds me a lot of my relationship with God. God fills my life with warmth and light, but He also causes the ugly floaty-things in my life to be very transparent.

God is holy, so as we grow in relationship with Him, our sins become more apparent. But that is why we must grasp onto grace! Grace allows us to have intimacy with a perfect God even in our imperfect state. Jesus died on the cross to give us His righteousness, so we could be dead to sin and alive in Christ.

"But if we walk in the light, as he is in the light, we have fellowship with one another, and the blood of Jesus, his Son, purifies us from all sin" (1 John 1.7 NIV).

Tragic Awakening

We usually take the important things in life for granted until tragedy strikes. Over eight years ago, I woke up in the middle of the night because something did not feel right. I got up and checked on my son, and he was fine. As I walked back to bed, the phone rang. It was a 3:00-o'clock-in-the-morning-something-is-wrong kind of phone call.

My brother-in-law was calling me with devastating news: my identical twin sister had been in a car wreck and was in critical condition. Her injuries were so severe she had to be helicoptered to the trauma center in San Antonio. I fell to my knees disbelieving the news. Two hours later, I rushed to San Antonio.

When I finally got there, I went straight to the emergency room. There I saw someone I had loved all my life on the verge of death. My twin sister's body was broken, and she was in intense pain. I asked the doctor if she was going to live, and he replied, "I don't know."

The pretense of security in my life vanished. I realized that family, health and the comforts of this world are all gifts that God has given me, and I deserve none of them. Life is so precious, and I couldn't believe how much I have taken it for granted.

Thankfully, my sister did live and underwent many months of

rehabilitation. She maintains several large scars, a metal hip and some nerve pain as evidence of her near-death accident. I will never take her for granted again. In fact, I daily strive to see the value of all God's blessings in my everyday life.

I thank God for allowing me to be a wife, a mother, a sister, a daughter and a friend every single day. When I focus on all that God has given me, I'm less worried about the things that truly don't matter.

"Teach us to number our days aright, that we may gain a heart of wisdom" (Psalm 90.12 NIV).

Too Good to be True

I bought a new chai mix. The one I normally use is a liquid, but this one came in a powder form. I glanced at the instructions, and it read that I can use three tablespoons of the dry mix for 8 ounces of water. I quickly filled my favorite mug with hot water, and scooped out three spoonfuls with the handy scooper they supplied within the jar. I tasted the finished result and discovered it was way too sweet for me.

I poured the chai into another mug and gave it to my husband. I figured that he wouldn't mind the extra sweet flavor. I went back to the kitchen and filled my mug once again with 8 ounces of hot water. This time I added only one heaping scoop of the chai mixture. I stirred the steaming liquid and took a sip. It tasted perfect! I was so excited! I only needed 1/3 of the required powder, so I would consume only 1/3 of the calories.

I looked at the nutritional label and discovered that the three tablespoons of chai mix equaled 150 calories, so I would take in only 50 calories for a yummy, frothy cup of chai tea latte! It seemed too good to be true! I have found the miracle beverage!

A few days later, I made another chai for my husband and me. I gave him only two scoops of chai mix this time because he said that the last one was too sweet for him. As I scooped out his second helping, my mind became a little suspicious. I held up the scooper and analyzed it.

I wondered if the scoop actually held the full three tablespoons of mixture required for the 8 ounces of chai. Sure enough, it did. My miracle beverage was actually a caloric nightmare!

In life, there are many things that are too good to be true, but the Good News of Jesus Christ is ALL GOOD and ALL TRUE! Jesus died for our sins and gave us His righteousness, so we could live for eternity in heaven with God. We don't have to be good enough, work hard enough or know enough; we simply need to accept the gift of salvation for our sins.

And the thing about Jesus is that we can never have too much of Him. In fact, the more we drink and eat of His Word and His goodness, the healthier—physically, emotionally, mentally and spiritually—we will become! An abundant life with Jesus may seem too good to be true, but it's a promise!

"The thief does not come except to steal, and to kill, and to destroy. I have come that they may have life, and that they may have it more abundantly" (John 10.10 NKJV).

The Day After

I look forward to the Christmas season like a snowman looks forward to the winter—I just can't wait until it arrives! I love watching old Christmas movies, listening to Christmas music on the radio, dressing up in red and green, going to Christmas parties and, most of all, I love Christmas traditions—baking cookies, sending Christmas cards, decorating the Christmas tree and opening presents.

I also enjoy driving around the city and looking at all of the Christmas decorations and lights on everyone's homes. It is so fun to connect the Christmas decorations with the people that live there. Some people decorate their homes with simple white lights, some people use colorful lights and some people go all out with a fake snowman, candy canes, reindeers and icicle lights.

It's so wonderful to see the homes that have big-lighted crosses or nativities in their yard. I remember driving to my house the day after Christmas several years ago. I saw all of the decorations and thought that they looked so depressing. They were a reminder that Christmas was over and I would have to wait another year to get back that Christmas spirit. Then it dawned on me. As a Christian, I didn't need to wait an entire year to have the Christmas spirit. I can have it all the time!

It didn't matter that I had to put all of my decorations back into storage for another twelve months. Christ came to this earth to give us an eternity with Him. I can keep the joy and wonderment of His birth with me every day. As a Christian, Christmas decorations could, theoretically, stay up at my house all year long. Christmas is more than just a holiday; it is the foundation of eternal life. We have the privilege to shine the Christmas spirit from our lips, actions and lives every moment all year long.

"Today in the town of David a Savior has been born to you; he is Christ the Lord" (Luke 2.11 NIV).

A Tack of Forgiveness

I remember as children my twin sister and I would wake up early in the morning and put tacks on the stairs. We would strategically place the tacks with the sharp points facing up where we thought someone would step on them. Then we would each hide on either side of the stairwell and watch as our groggy mother stepped on a tack, screamed out in pain and try to take the tack out of her foot while trying not fall down the stairs.

My twin and I would cover our mouths to try and stifle our mischievous laughs. We were horrible! I still can't believe we used to do that! We didn't fully realize at such a young age that hurting people was wrong. Years later we remembered our horrifying deed and asked our mother for forgiveness. I think back to this every time someone hurts me.

Many people hurt others; and for any number of reasons, they don't really comprehend that what they are doing is wrong. Hurting people hurt people, but healed people can help heal others through love and forgiveness. When someone hurts us, at some point we are going to have to let go of the pain and give it to God. If we are to go from hurt to healed, we need to forgive.

"To open their eyes and turn them from darkness to light, and from the power of Satan to God, so that they may receive forgiveness of sins and a place among those who are sanctified by faith in me" (Acts 26.18 NIV).

Running Circles

When I was about twenty-one years old, I was running on the track at the local athletic club. I was going pretty fast, so I stayed on the outside lane for runners. I remember passing a young teenager who was doing her very best in the inside lane. She was handicapped and pushed a walker in front of her. I ran past her many times during my three-mile jog.

I remember feeling sorry for her because she couldn't go very fast. Toward the end of my run, I wanted to get a good look at her face. I wanted to see the emotions she was feeling. As I looked at her, I was humbled. There was an expression of devoted determination on her face; and I realized that if she wasn't handicapped, she would have run circles around me. I was moved by the effort of her unwavering will.

As I have reflected on that moment, I've come to understand the destructiveness of comparisons. That young girl was probably putting more effort into her walk than I have ever put into any of my workouts. On the outside, it looked like I was achieving more; but in reality, she was progressing way more than I was. We compare ourselves with others without realizing the defeat in it. We can't compare our heart, our will, our determination, our loyalty—only God can do that. All we can compare is the physical effects, which vary and give little indication of what's inside of us.

If we compare, then we have judged others and ourselves based on extremely distorted information. It's a waste of time and energy! Comparing comes so naturally to us, but it's so freeing to just let it go. It allows us to stop asking ourselves, "Why can't I be more like her or have what she has?" and start asking, "God, will You help me achieve the beauty of Your unique design for me?"

"We do not dare to classify or compare ourselves with some who commend themselves. When they measure themselves by themselves and compare themselves with themselves, they are not wise" (2 Corinthians 10.12 NIV).

Rags to Robes

As Christians, we can choose to take a step of obedience or stay resolutely in our self-will. If we choose to be obedient, we find ourselves in a situation that is outside of our comfort zone. Insecurities and doubts begin to plague our minds. We may feel confused, lost, scared, anxious, unworthy, inept, uncomfortable and a dozen of other negative emotions. We may become frustrated because our step of obedience has stripped us of our carefully constructed image based on our own accomplishments.

God strips us of our worldly rags and offers us royal robes. But those royal robes scare us to death! Some of us never put them on and we demand our rags back. Others put the robes on, but they feel out of character. Many of us stand naked and exposed because we don't want to put our rags back on; yet, we will not put on the robes. We wallow in our despair and wonder why we are not fulfilling the purpose God has designed for us.

We need to stop wallowing, put on the robes and feel safe in the fact that we will quickly grow into them. We might feel like phonies at first; however, we will transform into the image God desires for us. But be careful! Once the robes really start to feel like a second skin, God will ask us to take another step of obedience into a brand-new set of robes. Be obedient to God, knowing that all of your worthiness comes from

Christ Jesus and not from yourself.

"Jesus replied, 'Anyone who loves me will obey my teaching. My Father will love them, and we will come to them and make our home with them'" (John 14.23 NIV).

Loving the Porcupine

When we read the scripture about loving our enemy, we might envision a deranged lunatic out to kill us. But in actuality our enemy is usually a person close to us: a boss or co-worker, a parent, an in-law, a son or daughter, a student, a friend or a spouse. This person may have consistently hurt us, or she may have hurt us only briefly. This person may have felt remorse for what she has done, or she may not have acknowledged it.

These people are porcupines because whenever we get close to them, we get hurt. Enemies come in every shade and hue, and it is impossible to understand their actions. But it is possible, however, to understand our actions. We are not accountable for any person's behavior besides our own. When God says to love your enemy, He wants us to love the co-worker who constantly belittles. He wants us to love that teenager who always disobeys. He wants us to love that parent who repeatedly condemns. He wants us to love that spouse who has given up.

God wants us to love with a heart that is always searching for the good in people. He wants us to love the porcupines in our lives, although loving them is never easy. Many times it's easier to focus on their negative characteristics. It takes motivated determination to filter through the coal to find the diamonds. We need to learn from Jesus' example, a sinless man who sacrificed His life for the love He has for humanity. So love the porcupines through Jesus Christ; and though they might not return the love, Jesus will in overflowing proportions.

"But I tell you: Love your enemy and pray for those who persecute you" (Matthew 5.44 NIV).

The Judging Trap

God convicted me about judging others. A judging spirit is one of the most incognito sins out there. It feels natural to give your opinion about others. Sometimes, it even feels like we have the right to speak our mind, but we don't. The only person that ever lived who has the right to judge is Jesus Christ.

God began to reveal my judgmental attitude, and I ardently began to stop myself. However, I still continued to judge those who have hurt me. It made the pain they caused more bearable to see that they had flaws and sins of their own. God quickly convicted me on that. He made it clear that I was to love those who judged and condemned me, and that their judgmental spirit did not justify mine.

Therefore, I fervently began to curb my judging attitude some more. Then, I started judging people who spoke against God. Anyone who said God didn't exist or who showed hatred towards Him, I judged. Consequently, God quickly remedied my prideful spirit by reminding me that He loved and died for ALL of us—not just believers.

Finally, because I had gotten so good at noticing judgmental attitudes, I began to judge people who judged. I started to say things like, "Did you hear her? She just judged that person" or "I can't believe she just pointed out the speck in that person's eye. How dare she!" I had fallen into the judging trap! God finally called me on it.

I found that there is freedom in a judge-free spirit. It is easier to love and serve others when we are not busily pointing out their sins. God is the supreme judge, and we are showing him disrespect and dishonor when we try to play His role. The fact is that we all have fallen short of the glory of God. Mercy and grace are so much easier to give others when we fully understand how much mercy and grace God has given us!

"There is only one Lawgiver and Judge, the one who is able to save and destroy. But you – who are you to judge your neighbor?" (James 4.12 NIV).

Amazing Grace

I was driving in my car listening to "Grace Like Rain" by Todd Agnew, which has some of the lyrics of John Newton's song "Amazing Grace" in it. And I wondered how Newton would react to the fact that parts of his song were being pulsed through radio waves in the sky, blasting through speakers of a self-moving contraption over 350 years later! Did he know that the time he took to sit down and write the song would influence so many lives? Could he have fathomed that the small effort of obedience he dedicated to God would make such a difference?

God says that the good work He has started in you will continue until His coming. That means that your good works do not die when you do. The people you influence and the sacrifices that you make today will continue even after you take your last breath. The deposits that you make into God's Kingdom will not fully mature until Jesus comes again.

So don't feel defeated when your good works have not been immediately followed by rewards. The love and sacrifice you show to your family, friends, acquaintances and strangers are being seen and are being tabulated. And when you see God face-to-face, He will reveal to you the wonderful and expanding effect that your small sacrifice produced.

"Being confident of this, that he who began a good work in you will carry it on to completion until the day of Christ Jesus" (Philippians 1.6 NIV).

Legacy Misunderstood

When I was 16, there was a girl in my church who I thought hated me. She seemed very rude and caustic with me. I always felt that she was making fun of me, and I thought that she just didn't care to be my friend. So I finally stopped trying to get to know her.

Fifteen years later, there is a man who owns a small café where I sometimes buy my coffee. He is sarcastic and many times seems rude, but I know he just has a personality that is different than mine. He's actually a pretty nice man once you get past his rough exterior. I overlook his jibes because I know that he is not trying to insult me; he's just trying to be friendly the only way he knows how.

One day as I was ordering my coffee, I saw the girl I knew when I was 16. She was talking with the owner of the café. He was making sarcastic remarks and trying to be funny and she was smiling. Every time he would say something rude, she would just laugh and say something rude back. They bantered back and forth for several minutes like this. The entire time the girl (now woman) had an expression of enjoyment on her face. I finally asked her, "Do you know this man?" She looked at me surprised and said, "Yes. He is my father."

Fireworks went off in my head. For fifteen years, I thought this girl didn't like me. I thought she was rude and was constantly judging me.

But I realized it was I who was judging her. She didn't hate me. She merely related to me the best way she knew how, and I was too self-focused and insecure to understand her. I should have tried to see life through her eyes and not spotlight my own feelings. Maybe then we could have forged a stronger, Christ-centered relationship.

Now I know that I miss out on sharing God's love and making those meaningful connections when I constantly worry about my own feelings. It is so much easier to love others when I'm focused on how they feel, rather than getting caught up in my own self-centered emotions. I want to make an effort to give people the benefit of the doubt and not let my insecurities get in the way of seeing the best in people. I'm determined to see the image of Christ in others.

"A fool shows his annoyance at once, but a prudent man overlooks an insult" (Proverbs 12.16 NIV).

Achieving Our Throne

Sometimes I become impatient with God's promises. He has designed each of us for a specific purpose; and if we listen intently enough, we will come to understand that purpose. But why doesn't God bring that purpose to fruition right away? Why must we obediently wait on the path to that purpose forging our way through circumstances, people and situations that seem wholly unrelated?

When I ask these questions in frustration, I think of King David. God promised King David in his youth that he would be king of all Israel, but David had to wait many years and endure many challenges before his throne was realized. Why didn't God immediately serve the throne to David on a silver platter? David's character was not yet ready to bear the burden of responsibilities that came with the throne.

We all have our own throne (purpose) promised to us by God, but the process of preparation takes time. Our character needs to be ready to bear the weight of the responsibilities that come with our promised destiny. I have not yet reached my throne, but I know that I'm on the right path. I have realized that the difficult circumstances God has allowed on my path have been preparing me for the mighty work He has for me.

So instead of complaining to God with impatience, I pray to God that I may learn, grow and change during the uncomfortable and difficult situations, so that someday I may fulfill my purpose in a way that is pleasing to Him. He's teaching me that if I rely on Him, I can accomplish everything He has called me to. When I do come to my own personal throne, I will rejoice and dance like David, and I will not take that purpose for granted.

"O Lord my God, you have performed many wonders for us. Your plans for us are too numerous to list. You have no equal. If I tried to recite all your wonderful deeds, I would never come to the end of them" (Psalm 40.5 NLT).

Rebuke Me

I was talking to my twin sister about a concern I had with a particular topic. She wisely told me that my opinion might be judgmental and that I should probably keep it to myself. I was upset at first because I thought, *Surely, my opinion is godly and right.* However, her loving rebuke stayed in my mind; and throughout the next several days, I came into contact with three different friends on separate occasions.

This particular topic that my sister advised me on came up. Though my opinion popped into my head—and I still as of yet didn't see a problem with it—I kept it to myself. During the conversation with each friend, I had a chance to voice my "godly and right" opinion, but I respected my sister's judgment and I trusted her counsel. In retrospect, I realized that though my opinion was "right" for me, it wasn't necessarily right for others.

I discovered that I was transferring the Holy Spirit's will towards my life onto my friends. What was a godly yoke for me would have been a religious burden for someone else. I am so thankful that I listened to my sister, and I am proud of myself that I didn't allow my feelings to get in the way of God's protection. I will never be perfect, and I will always make mistakes, but I will continually be on the lookout for God's reprimand because I know that He is trying to prepare me for victory ahead.

"Timely advice is lovely, like golden apples in a silver basket" (Proverbs 25.11 NLT).

Transitions in the Road

I had to put my rollerblading on hold for about six years while my husband and I were growing our family. I enjoyed rollerblading a lot in my twenties, and it was so nice to finally be able to strap on my blades and hit the pavement. It took me several days of skating for my body and mind to remember how it was done.

I also noticed that I was a lot more careful skating than when I was in my twenties. I have a lot more responsibilities as a wife, mother and Jesus disciple; and I have people counting on me. Though I know life will go on as usual even if I did get hurt, I wasn't going to purposely jump into any life-halting accidents.

As I rollerbladed, I was very careful during the transitions in the road. When the sidewalk gave way to the street, there were lots of bumps and rocks on my path. I had to focus my eyes directly on the terrain in front of me and slow down so I wouldn't fall. Once I crossed the street and continued back on the sidewalk, I was able to look to the horizon and skate faster. Right before skating through another intersection, I felt the Holy Spirit say, "Be careful during the transitions in the road."

God knows me so well. I tend to get an idea of God's vision for me and charge full steam ahead. However, when my life is in transition, I need to be cautious. I must pray about every detail because the enemy puts out many stumbling blocks when he thinks we are not looking. The enemy doesn't want us to change and grow. He wants us to fall flat on our faces and give up.

Transitions in our spiritual walk are very special. They signify a growth into Christlikeness; however, they are a bit chaotic. As God entrusts us with more, we need to spend more time seeking Him. As Christ-followers, people are looking to us for guidance. When we see a transition in the road, we need to keep our eyes focused on God. God protects our paths and guides our steps, so we can be a strong witness to the world.

"He holds victory in store for the upright, he is a shield to those whose walk is blameless, for he guards the course of the just and protects the way of his faithful ones" (Proverbs 2.7-8 NIV).

Power of the Flash Drive

For some reason my computer would not read my camera card. Every time I would stick the tiny disk into the USB port, the computer refused to open my picture folder. I'd have to put the card back into my camera and continue taking my family photos. However, after several weeks and dozens of photo ops, my camera was jam-packed with beautiful memories; and I desperately needed to upload them to my family blog—the grandparents were waiting!

So I decided to put the pictures on my laptop, save them to a disk and upload them to my home computer. I forgot how large photo and video files were because the entire process took about an hour and used up a dozen CDs. Finally, when I tried to put the last video on a CD, the file was too large. The video could not be uploaded.

I was so frustrated because I couldn't finish this already aggravating project that I started. I went upstairs and accidentally discovered my husband's flash drive. I plugged it into the laptop, cautiously put all the files on it and pushed save. It worked! As the files were being transferred, I was reminded that when we try to accomplish goals in our own strength; we will only find ourselves frustrated and inadequate. But when we tap into God's strength, we will find an endless supply of power, resources and ability.

"But Jesus looked at them and said, 'With men this is impossible, but all things are possible with God'" (Matthew 19.26 AMP).

Fellowship of the Mice

My sister's garage door broke one night, and mice got into her house. Since her husband was away on business, she and her three little ones had to live with mice for several days. She was miserable. She put out traps, she searched her house for foul-smelling carcasses, and she went to bed with visions of rodents in her head.

She called me crying, so I went into action and obtained reinforcements. There was no reason why my sister had to face this mouse menace alone. My brother, my sister-in-law and I all went to my sister's house. Just having us there made her feel so much better. We told our stories of rodent woes and helped looked for the smelly remains.

My sister's mood instantly brightened once she realized that she wasn't alone. There were people around her who loved her and who wanted to help her through the fuzzy predicament. We all had a good laugh, and we got to encourage and uplift each other. It was such a wonderful time!

Isn't it interesting how fellowship can change a yucky situation into something enjoyable? Knowing that we are not alone can make all the difference in the world. When we walk in love, caring for the needs of others, we gain a clearer picture of Christ's love for us. We can trust that during this life, God will never forsake us or leave us. We can make it through the tough times because Jesus is right here with us.

"And walk in love, [esteeming and delighting in one another] as Christ loved us and gave Himself up for us, a slain offering and sacrifice to God [for you, so that it became] a sweet fragrance" (Ephesians 5.2 AMP).

Iced Tea

When I was around 8 years old, I went to a friend's house for the first time. His mother was very pleasant and hospitable. She asked if I would like a glass of iced tea. I kindly declined, saying that I didn't like iced tea. This woman took my words as a challenge, and she quickly went into the kitchen to brew and flavor her "special" recipe.

When she handed me the beautifully prepared glass of her favorite beverage, she made sure to tell me that the tea had several different kinds of freshly squeezed fruit and plenty of spoonfuls of sugar in it. I took one sip and scrunched my nose. The sugar and fruit tasted good, but I wasn't accustomed to the earthy flavor of tea.

The woman looked very disappointed when I handed the cup back to her. It took me over twenty-five years, but I finally started liking the inherent flavors of tea. I wish I could find that nice lady and ask for another glass. I'm sure this time I would savor the lovely cup of her special brew!

As Christians, we can present the Gospel in beautiful, creative and amazing ways; but if the receivers dislike the taste of the Holy Spirit, there is no special recipe that will change their preference. People need to be open to the movement of the Holy Spirit if they are going to embrace the Good News of Jesus Christ. As Disciples of Christ, we can do our best to present the Truth to others, but if they reject the Holy Spirit, we can only pray that someday (even twenty-five years later) His presence will taste sweet to them.

"There's nothing done or said that can't be forgiven. But if you deliberately persist in your slanders against God's Spirit, you are repudiating the very One who forgives. If you reject the Son of Man out of some misunderstanding, the Holy Spirit can forgive you, but when you reject the Holy Spirit, you're sawing off the branch on which you're sitting, severing by your own perversity all connection with the One who forgives" (Matthew 12.31-32 MSG).

Shout of the Healed

I saw a friend tonight stand up in front of the crowd declaring God's love. The joy, power and comfort of God surrounded her. His light reflected from her and mingled with the fire of Christ burning within her. I knew I was staring, but I couldn't help it. She blazed with God's goodness.

"His Goodness," I thought! She was diagnosed with breast cancer only days ago, and she BLAZED with God's goodness! This woman who has every right to claim fear, mistrust and hurt has never looked so loved, so protected and so comforted. "I will get to know my God as the Great Healer!" she exclaimed.

When she said those words, my spirit felt a tinge of jealousy. She will know God in an intimate way that I've never known. God has healed me from many things, but I've never feared for my life. How beautiful to watch God prove Himself with your life! How intimately wonderful to trust Him with your very breath!

She knows that He is not done with her, and she is ready to experience this path that He has laid out for her. She walks a silent road that would cripple most, yet she has the strength to move forward. She walks with victory in her hands and faith guiding her every step. She sees this new journey as a glorious adventure, and her confidence makes me love and trust my God even more!

"Shouts of joy and victory resound in the tents of the righteous: 'The LORD's right hand has done mighty things!'" (Psalm 118.15 NIV).

Romanticized Obedience

Lately, God has been prompting me to do many things that I do not understand. As I take each step of obedience, I can't help but analyze and romanticize the results. I imagine this awesome outcome that shines the glory of God and affects many lives. I anticipate the gates of heaven opening up, flooding the fruits of my efforts with miraculous and jaw-dropping wonders. However, the endings that I dream up usually fizzle away, and I'm left with conclusions that wouldn't make it into a book, let alone a best-seller's list.

After one such disappointing end to a much built up step of obedience, I asked God what I was doing wrong. Clearly, I was messing something up or not fully understanding God's whispers into my heart. Although I'm sure that God appreciated my version of the story, I can't help but think He must have been quite amused. He finally showed me what I was missing: Everything!

He told me that I have a very limited perspective of my life, so I cannot fully comprehend the beautiful story that He is weaving for me. He also told me that when I do know the eternal scope of my time on earth and the outcome of all my steps of obedience are laid before me, I will fall to my knees in awe of the miraculous and jaw-dropping wonder that He created through my obedience and trust in Him. I want to trust that God is planting great beauty in my life even when I don't always see it.

"How foolish can you be? He is the Potter, and he is certainly greater than you, the clay! Should the created thing say of the one who made it, 'He didn't make me'? Does a jar ever say, 'The potter who made me is stupid'?" (Isaiah 29.16 NLT).

Deeper Roots

As I was walking toward the building, I prayed for a freak natural disaster to occur—like a tornado or maybe an earthquake. No one would get hurt, of course; but the normal day would be disrupted. When nothing happened and each step took me closer to the entrance, I prayed desperately for God to send a whale to swallow me whole. I wanted to be like Jonah hiding in a waterlogged belly rather than obediently walking up the steps of the English building.

I was twenty-five years old and about to teach my first college composition class. I wore a three-piece suit and carried a briefcase by my side, and I felt like a big, fat phony. Why was God making me do something He knew was way over my head? Why did He design me to be introverted only to push me into the center of attention? Why did being obedient to God always require so much forced resolve?

Eleven years later, I don't know the exact reasons why God directed me on a teaching path, but I do know that I am a better person because of my obedience. God has asked me to do many things that are outside my comfort zone, and each step of obedience has grown my roots deeper in Him. Sometimes I have had to just shut down my emotions and cling to the knowledge that God knows what He is doing.

I wish I could interact with the young woman from my past whose face had fear written all over it. Before she closed the door of security behind her and walked nervously to the front of her first class; I would smile, look into her fearful eyes and say, "Thank you for your obedience; because of it, I am proud of who I am today." I also might add, "Wow! You look great in that suit."

"But Samuel replied: 'Does the Lord delight in burnt offerings and sacrifices as much as in obeying the voice of the Lord? To obey is better than sacrifice, and to heed is better than the fat of rams'" (1 Samuel 15.22 NIV).

The Gears of Grace

Lately, I've taking up cycling at the gym. I really enjoy my spin class because I can zone out and let my brain relax. I'm not going anywhere on my stationary bike, so I don't have to worry about my surroundings. I just pick up the speed, change my gears and sit and stand when my instructor tells me to. By the time I leave, my body and mind are purged and refreshed.

By now I've learned my settings for the different terrain scenarios we ride. I know what gears I need to take it easy, to race and to pedal standing. I can gage my body and energy level and push myself to make the ride hard or relax on the gears and make my ride easy. One particular day, I decided that I was going to take my cycling workout to the next level. I wanted to increase my gears by 1 or 2 points during every song, so I could raise the intensity of my ride and test my endurance.

When the music started, I noticed that my normal "ride easy" gear was tough. I felt like I was in my racing gear. Then when I set my racing gear, I felt like I was in my climbing gear. Not only could I not set new highs for my gear settings, I had to back off on the gears just to be able to finish each ride. By the end of the course, I was worn out and disappointed. I wondered if I had lost some stamina over the weekend.

I talked to one of the ladies who had been taking the spin class for years about my frustrating ride. She smiled with understanding and quickly explained that a few of the bikes' gears were not working properly. She said that the gear settings were off and that they needed to be fixed by the equipment specialist. I felt a little relieved, but I wanted to wait until my next class to guarantee that it wasn't my stamina that was the problem.

Two days later, I made sure to get on another bike. I tested my normal gear settings and discovered that the woman was right: the bike I rode earlier was off—way off! I decided to push myself during that spin class and broke all my previous gear setting highs. It was so nice to see an honest display of how much I have improved.

As I finished the class, I felt the Holy Spirit tell me something important. It wasn't really said in words; instead, He imparted some of His understanding into my heart. What I discovered is that as Christians, God's favor and grace automatically place us on higher gears. While everyone trudges through life without the guidance of the Holy Spirit (John 16.13) and the renewed mind of Christ (Romans 12.2), Christians have an intrinsic wind that pushes and directs them on a life of purpose, power and meaning—if they are willing to seek and receive it.

I believe that if Christians were to seek God daily and bring all their thoughts, decisions and actions to His throne, God would place us on the fastest, surest and strongest path to achieving our destiny. We would lose all idle time and fully embrace each day that He has given us. And as we spend time with God, we will realize that our purest joy is found in our intimacy with Him. We will fully understand how blessed we are to have an eternal relationship with our Creator who loves and enjoys us. And every day will be filled with hope and joy because our sins have been cleansed by Jesus who died to give us eternal life with God.

"He is so rich in kindness and grace that he purchased our freedom with the blood of his Son and forgave our sins" (Ephesians 1.7 NLT).

Pink Slippers

When I was a little girl, I almost never wore shoes. I didn't see the need for them. But when I rode my bike, I had to scrounge up a pair. The pedals of my bike had jagged prongs on them, and they would hurt my bare feet.

I remember one sunny morning I really wanted to ride my bike. I was eight years old, and I had places to explore! I looked for a pair of shoes and found little pink slippers. I didn't know whose they were, but they might have been hand-me-downs. I slipped them on, and I felt feminine and beautiful. I tiptoed out the front door like a ballerina.

I hopped on my bike and leisurely rode around my block. I took in the soft summer breeze and the early morning glow of the sun. I coasted to an intersection, got off my bike and waited for the light to turn green. There was another little girl on the sidewalk waiting to cross the street with me. She was a few years older than I was. She stared at me for a good while then looked at my slippers and said, "Nice shoes."

I looked down at my slippers and analyzed what she saw. Until this day, I still have the image of them in my mind. Although it was obvious they were once pink, they had turned a brownish color with dirty smudges across the plastic sides. There was a hole where my right big toe was and you could see my toe sticking out. The seams where the plastic tops were sewn to the soles were unraveling. The strap across the top of the left slipper was broken. I think about them now and realize that they should have been thrown away years ago.

Because I had no clue what sarcasm was, I thought the little girl was being genuine with her compliment. I stared back up at her face and beamed a smile, "Thank you," I said. "These are my new slippers."

The girl looked at me for a moment longer, chuckled and walked off.

I had found a treasure, and I was so pleased someone else had noticed. In my childish mind, I only knew that the slippers were beautiful. It didn't matter to me the condition of them.

And you are beautiful to the Creator. He has made you into His treasure and it doesn't matter what the world has put you through or what kind of condition you find yourself in. You are valuable simply because You are His.

God doesn't see the smudges, the holes or the unraveling seams; He only sees you—His beautiful slippers. Why? Because God came into this world in the form of a man, taught us how to love, and took the ugliness of our lives. Jesus Christ completely erases our sin, so God only sees beauty. If you don't feel beautiful, worthy or valued; then you might be viewing yourself through the world's eyes. See yourself through God's eyes, and you'll wake up every morning feeling like the treasure you were created to be.

"For we are God's masterpiece. He has created us anew in Christ Jesus, so we can do the good things he planned for us long ago" (Ephesians 2.10 NLT).

The Language of God

A language that is actively being spoken transforms. Only dead languages, like Latin, stay the same as the years roll by. English is no different. There is a remarkable difference between Chaucer's Old English, Shakespeare's Early Modern English and today's English. New English words are being formed every year, especially with the advancement of technology. Words unheard of less than ten years ago, like Blog, Tweet and Wi-Fi, are now commonplace.

As language is being used, the pronunciation of words also changes. The vowel sounds shift, and some vowels become long, while others become silent. Groupings of consonances begin to take on unique articulations, and words no longer sound the same. To compensate, teachers and grammarians make up little rules to help their learners understand the different sounds. But the fact is that "e" doesn't really make the "a" long, and people once pronounced the "ght" in "knight" (sounds like you are clearing your throat). Our language morphed into something different to embrace the people communicating it.

For this reason, people say that language is a living thing. The same is true for God's Living Word, the Bible. Yes, the stories were written thousands of years ago, but there is something living and active about the words tucked in between Genesis and Revelation. Originally written in Hebrew (Old Testament) and Greek (New Testament), the

Bible has renewed itself in fresh ways (at times with much difficulty and persecution) to embrace the people currently communicating on this earth.

Even though the Bible has changed from King James Version to the multitude of translations and languages we have today, the heart of the Bible is still the same. The Bible is about a Creator in love with His Creation and willing to do anything—including dying for the sins that separate Him from His beloved—to draw them into relationship with Him for eternity. And language, diction, grammar, spelling and vocabulary will not stop God from reaching those He prizes most–US!

Jesus loves you is such a simple phrase, but this little phrase is the scarlet thread woven through the entire Bible. Therefore, when you read every psalm, proverb, narrative, parable and prophecy, just remember that phrase: Jesus loves you. The Holy Spirit in every Christian is an amazing teacher, and He will help you through the grammar, spelling and pronunciation, so you can read the Heart of God and believe His Word.

"For the word of God is quick, and powerful, and sharper than any two-edged sword, piercing even to the dividing asunder of soul and spirit, and of the joints and marrow, and is a discerner of the thoughts and intents of the heart" (Hebrews 4.12 KJV).

Strength in Weakness

I have nodules (calluses) on my vocal cords. Singers get these due to the stress of singing. These nodules cause your voice to sound breathy and hoarse. I grew up going to speech therapy, and my distinct voice sparked my immense fear of public speaking.

To my chagrin, God called me to public speaking. The week before my first speaking assignment, I was so consumed by anxiety and worry that I literally could not sleep. It was the worst case of insomnia that I've ever had in my life!

Little did I know that my perceived weakness would force me to be innovative. I grabbed at anything that would divert my audience's attention away from me. I learned and implemented computer software, utilized original visual aids, created exciting group work and interweaved the Internet into my talks. If I could just keep the minds of my audience continuously busy, then I wouldn't have to worry about them analyzing me and my voice!

Flash forward ten years later. I completed a speaking assignment last night; and as I watched my audience members smile and laugh; discuss problems and answers; encourage one another and talk like old friends, I was amazed. This was our first meeting, yet my audience interacted like we had been meeting for years. Needless to say, none of them got bored or fell asleep! I spoke with confidence, and it felt good to know that I might be making a difference in their lives.

I realize now that I'm a pretty good speaker, and I'm also a very versatile speaker. My mind is constantly looking for ways to engage the audience and get them involved. My testimony about my speaking journey always blows people away. But really it is all to the glory of God because everything is from Him. The only thing that I added to the mix was my *obedience*. My obedience in my weakness caused me to be innovative and propelled God's strength in my life!

Working with a weakness is difficult, but it helps us to rely solely on God. I'm reminded of 2 Corinthians 12.9: "But he said to me, 'My grace is sufficient for you, for my power is made perfect in weakness.' Therefore, I will boast all the more gladly about my weaknesses, so that Christ's power may rest on me" (NIV). God gives us weaknesses for a reason. They force us out of our limited expectations and help us to look for new possibilities!

If you feel God calling you to work inside of a weakness, be excited! He is about to do something amazing in your life. Though the path will not be easy, trust that God knows what He is doing. He will not ask you to do anything unless He has declared your victory. Repeat the following list out loud and take that step of obedience. Your weakness can become one of your greatest assets!

1. My weakness will cause me to be innovative
2. My weakness will give me a unique perspective
3. God will use my weakness to show His glory
4. God will do something new in my weakness
5. God gives me victory in my weakness
6. God gives me grace (supernatural favor) in my weakness
7. "I can do everything through him who gives me strength" (Philippians 4.13 NIV).

Now go claim those promises and change the world!

The Acts Get Up

Peter and Paul both healed a crippled man in Acts. I heard Peter's performance of healing while driving in the car. I just happened to flip to my audio Bible in my 5 CD changer and listened as Peter pulled a crippled man to his feet.

That same night when I was reading my one-year Bible before bed, I read about Paul's performance of healing. Paul yelled across a crowd of people for the crippled man to stand up, and he did.

Read both accounts quickly and see if you can notice the difference.

First:

"When he saw Peter and John about to enter the Temple, he [the crippled man] asked for a handout. Peter, with John at his side, looked him straight in the eye and said, 'Look here.' He looked up, expecting to get something from them. Peter said, 'I don't have a nickel to my name, but what I do have, I give you: In the name of Jesus Christ of Nazareth, walk!' He grabbed him by the right hand and pulled him up. In an instant, his feet and ankles became firm. He jumped to his feet and walked" (Acts 3.5-8 MSG).

Second:

"There was a man in Lystra who couldn't walk. He sat there, crippled since the day of his birth. He heard Paul talking, and Paul, looking him in the eye, saw that he was ripe for God's work, ready to believe. So he said, loud enough for everyone to hear, "Up on your feet!" The man was up in a flash—jumped up and walked around as if he'd been walking all his life" (Acts 14.8-10 MSG).

The day that I happened to read these two healings, I was struggling. I was smack in the middle of a "crippling" season, and I wanted to claim defeat. Several so-called negative things happened in my life, and I wanted to crawl in a hole and disappear. I didn't want to get up. I wanted to get out!

After I read the second healing, God asked me a simple question: "Which one are you?"

During the tough times, was I going to be the man who was looking for a hand-out and had to be yanked up out of his crippled-ness? Or was I going to be the man "ripe for God's work" and by faithful determination jumped out of his crippled-ness?

God accomplishes His will either way. He can either pull us up when we've been knocked down or we can jump up claiming God's promised victory (Psalm 118.15)

I have made a vow to God. I want to be the second man. When I mess up or when bad things happen, I want to jump up and keep running the race. I trust that God uses all things (good and bad) to accomplish His perfect plan (Romans 8.28).

I've pursued Him, always trying to stay one step ahead of defeat. There was always another path to take—another way to make myself worthy of His blessing. And the result of this self-disciplined journey leads to the same end: I am nothing without God; everything comes from Him, through Him and to Him (Romans 11.36).

"For the LORD is good. His unfailing love continues forever, and his faithfulness continues to each generation" (Psalm 100.5 NLT).

God's love stays true even when I mess up. God's promises remain fixed even when I'm tired. God's Word stands firm even when I falter. My life is tucked inside the death, burial and resurrection of Jesus; and His holiness is mine because He claimed my sin as His own. So I move the faith I have placed in my corner and stake it all on Jesus. He is my only winning bet.

I hide from God when I look my worse, but He takes me by the face and demands that I see His love for me has not changed.

"So we have come to know and to believe the love that God has for us. God is love, and whoever abides in love abides in God, and God abides in him" (1 John 4.16 ESV).

Soul Sore

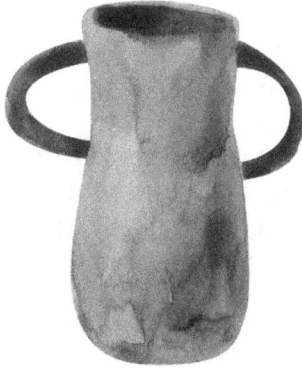

When I was in elementary school, I cried one afternoon because I didn't feel well. My teacher sent me to the nurse's office, which I had never been to before. The nurse was very sweet and asked me what the matter was. I told her that my entire body ached, and I didn't feel very well.

She pressed her hand against my forehead and took my temperature, but I didn't have a fever. She looked for other symptoms, but I had no congestion, coughing, runny nose, vomiting, diarrhea or sweating. The nurse was stumped, but she could tell I was being sincere about how I felt.

I remember her looking into my eyes, sensing my distress, and instantly making a decision. She called my mother to pick me up from school and take me home. She told me to lie down on the bed that was fitted with a clean, white sheet. I instantly reclined my sore, tender body, closed my eyes and waited for my mom to arrive. It wasn't until I was in high school that I realized what had happened to me way back then.

Our high school gymnasium had a long rope hanging from the ceiling to the floor. We had to climb that rope as part of an athletic challenge. All my life, I had been athletically driven, so I climbed thirty feet to the top and rung the tiny bell that was fastened to the ceiling.

I had mastered this feat many times, including in elementary school.

I woke up the next morning, and my entire body ached. I could barely move, let alone get out of bed. I finally had to rock my poor frame out from under the sheets and drag my weary bones to the shower. I needed hot water to relax my tense muscles.

As the heat penetrated my skin, I remembered my time at the nurse's office in elementary school. I distinctly recalled finishing a fitness test during P.E. the previous day. Suddenly, after many years had passed, I realized why I felt sick when I was a child: my entire body was sore from climbing the gym rope to the top!

God often has us climb great heights of faith for Him. We use up our strength and give Him all we've got. We finally make it to the top and ring our little bells of victory, but the next day we may feel spiritually worn out—like our souls are sore.

Oftentimes, we worry that something is wrong with us. Maybe we have an emotional ailment that is plaguing our lives. But I think many times we are simply tired and in need of a hot shower and a warm bed.

After achieving a difficult task for God's Kingdom, our souls may be a little tender and sensitive. Instead of grabbing hold of the next big adventure, we can take a little time to rest and recoup. It is difficult to serve others and run the race of faith when we are on the verge of tears. Rather than charging head-first into the next spiritual challenge, we can lay our weary heads at the foot of the throne and call our Abba Father to pick us up.

"Come to Me, all of you who work and have heavy loads. I will give you rest. Follow My teachings and learn from Me. I am gentle and do not have pride. You will have rest for your souls" (Matthew 11.28-29 NLV).

Gospel Shoes

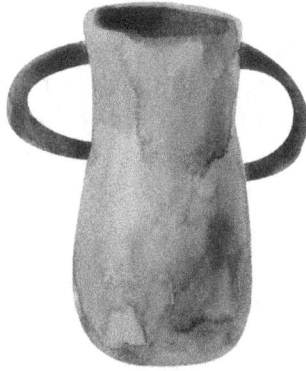

"Do you not know that in a race all the runners run, but only one gets the prize? Run in such a way as to get the prize. Everyone who competes in the games goes into strict training. They do it to get a crown that will not last, but we do it to get a crown that will last forever" (1 Corinthians 9.24-25 NIV).

During my sophomore year of high school, I ran track. Sadly, my new school didn't offer the sports I was good at (softball and volleyball), so I decided to kick my running legs into high gear. I grabbed my running shoes and hit the red-graveled track of my school.

Little did I know, however, that I didn't have running shoes. I had street shoes. I wasn't aware of this difference, so I ran my little heart out in those white, flat-soled shoes. I was fairly fast, and I could keep a quick pace for a good distance, so the coach had me run the mile relay (once around the track), the 400 (once around the track) and the 800 (twice around the track).

Before my first track meet, my mother offered to help buy me new shoes. I paid half and she paid half. I was shocked at how expensive running shoes were, and I wondered if they were worth emptying my pockets for. My last practice before our first competition, the coach had us run a mile to warm up. I flew past everyone and hit my fastest time running the mile. I was shocked. I wasn't even trying to race!

As I ran, I couldn't help imagining that I was a long-legged rabbit, jumping from one billowy cloud to the next. With every step, I felt my feet fly into the air, like I was wearing springs. I was amazed at what a difference a pair of shoes could make. I must have looked crazy to everyone because I was running with a big smile on my face. Two months of running with street shoes made running with real running shoes feel like a walk in the park!

The Bible compares our walk of faith to a race (2 Timothy 4.7). It also tells us that we should put on the shoes of the Gospel of Peace (Ephesians 6.15). So I've decided that if I'm going to be running this race for Christ, I want the right shoes on! The Shoes of Peace are not to benefit the onlookers; they are to benefit us, the runners!

When people see us flying by them with big, goofy smiles on our faces, they are going to take notice and wonder what makes us so different. The answer is JESUS and His Good News, the Gospel!

Street shoes represent running in our own strength and running for our own reasons. Yes, we can still run fast. Yes, we still can be productive. But we won't have the abundant peace that comes from resting in God's strength and knowing that we are fulfilling our God-given destiny!

We won't have the spring in our step that comes from the FREE and extra-cushy running shoes that Jesus Himself has purchased for us. Jesus gave His life for us so we could run this race for Him, and we can't squander this gift by ignoring the peace, joy, hope and strength that is found in the Gospel!

So don't try to run this race bare foot—without the Good News of eternal purpose and meaning. Remember that you are not alone. You are not forgotten. There is a reason for this life. God has great plans for you. We are saved from hopelessness and eternal separation from God.

We are forgiven from every sin. We have so much to celebrate and to be thankful for. Every promise is assured in Christ, and the bumps along the way won't even touch us. We are prepared with our Gospel Shoes, and we will run this race to win the honor of pleasing the King. When everything is said and done, we will be a crown of beauty in God's hand (Isaiah 62.3).

"And having shod your feet in preparation [to face the enemy with the firm-footed stability, the promptness, and the readiness produced by the good news] of the Gospel of peace" (Ephesians 6.15 AMP).

Keeping Secrets

Jesus' mother could definitely keep a secret. She spoke to angels, became pregnant as a virgin, was blessed by prophets, received gifts from Magi and escaped the genocide of firstborn sons. By the time she was still a young woman, she had a life filled with miracle memories surrounding the birth of the world's Messiah and her Son, Jesus. But instead of divulging her astounding secrets, the Bible says that Mary treasured them up in her heart (Luke 2.19).

People usually explore the negative aspects of sharing secrets (e.g. gossip, judgment, strife, etc.), but the Holy Spirit has been teaching me about the positive aspects of keeping secrets. I don't think it's a coincidence that God chose Mary—probably the best secret keeper in all of history—to raise the Baby of our Hope and Salvation.

As a writer, keeping secrets is difficult. I can make a God-moment out of almost any situation, and I love to spin stories into learning moments with the Holy Spirit. I might be introverted in person, but on paper, I am an open book with plenty to say. But I'm realizing that some secrets are too good to share. Some, in fact, will benefit me far more if I treasure them up.

The secrets I want to focus on are the ones where we follow the prompting of the Holy Spirit and God does something uniquely wonderful. We go out of our way to make a sacrifice and someone is blessed in return. Many times, God uses those stories to edify others, so there is nothing wrong with sharing them. However, I think that if we follow the Holy Spirit's leading, a few of those stories can be tucked into our hearts as seeds for God to bless.

The Bible says that anything we do in secret God will reward us in the open (Matthew 6.1-4). I don't know about you, but I would much rather be blessed by God than by people. I've decided to open the treasure chest of my heart and start placing my God-moments inside. I don't share them on Facebook. I don't write about them on my blog. I don't tell my closest confidante. Nope. I just store them up and let God do the rest.

I think God loves those little seeds of goodness, because He gets to grow them into awesome demonstrations of His glory. The seeds are planted into His eternal domain, and He can convey His love for us and show off His brilliant creativity on this earth. God has given us so many beautiful moments. Why not hold a couple of them back just for Him?

"Give your gifts in private, and your Father, who sees everything, will reward you" (Matthew 6.4 NLT).

What Shall I Wear?

Early one morning, I stared into my closet and wondered what I should wear. I was about to pull one of my nice shirts off of the hanger, but I thought better of it. I didn't want to waste a nice shirt on a day that was a "just-get-it-over-with" kind of day. "Today is not special," I thought. "I should just wear jeans and a t-shirt."

I put on the jeans and t-shirt and inspected myself in the mirror. I realized that I pretty much wear jeans and a t-shirt every day. As I stared at my reflection, God nicely connected my outward attire to my attitude. I had a negative attitude towards this day. I wanted to hurry up and get it out of the way. I had already made up my mind that this day would be unimportant and absolutely no fun. And judging from my hamper overflowing with t-shirts and jeans, I harbored that attitude a lot.

Although there is nothing wrong with wearing jeans and a t-shirt, God revealed an expectation and attitude I had about my days that needed to be readjusted. Every morning, I'd roll up my sleeves and plow through my day like a tractor on autopilot. I'd trudge along and miss most of the enjoyment because my expectations were low and my attitude was wrong.

Have you ever done that?

Have you ever thought to yourself, "If only I could get through this day, life would be better"?

God is teaching me that I need to change my attitude and expect great things every day. God is the master weaver of our days, and He does not waste a single one. None of our days drop under His radar; He has a divine appointment for us each and every day!

Now, I'm not saying that every day is going to be filled with rainbows and lollipops, but each day does serve a purpose. I think if we put our trust in God, we can find joy even in the hard times. God doesn't waste a single heartache, conflict or tragedy. He cares about us and our days, and He wants us to be blessed.

If you are a Christian, you have the ultimate portal to joy—Jesus Christ! People are looking at us, and they are wondering why we are here on this earth. They want to see if Jesus makes a difference in our lives. They need to see our joy, especially during the mundane and hard times.

If we start tapping into the joy that is within us, we would have joy everywhere we go, no matter the circumstance! Once we get good at opening that joy, we can start sharing it with those around us. We can pass out God's joy freely, and people will praise God because of it!

I am learning to put on a new attitude every morning, even if I still put on my jeans and t-shirt!

"This is the day the LORD has made; we will rejoice and be glad in it" (Psalm 118.24 NLT).

Corrupted Heart Systems

"Create in me a pure heart, O God, and renew a steadfast spirit within me" (Psalm 51.10 NIV).

My computer of many years crashed (smoke and all), so my husband bought me another computer right when a new programming system came out. I was so excited! I knew I would have to adjust to the new system, but I was sure that I would be just as efficient if not more so when I got the hang of it. Little did I know….

At first, everything on my computer screen looked somewhat familiar but misplaced. I had to search for the programs I used, and I had difficulty accessing the Internet. My music, photos, word files and other documents were all tucked away in mysterious places, and I had trouble finding them. However, as I began to use my computer for the various day-to-day tasks of life, things went from bad to worse.

I couldn't create or print labels. I couldn't print online tickets. I couldn't let my kids play their learning games online. I couldn't upload any of the photos from my phone. And if my computer was idle for more than five minutes, I couldn't access any of the windows that I had just opened. I couldn't research, create or produce. I was no longer efficient on the computer; I was positively ineffective!

I was conflicted because I couldn't tell if my problems were occurring because I wasn't getting it or if there was something wrong with my computer.

I finally called tech support, and the man on the other line took control of my computer. As I watched him search through my files, he finally pulled up a screen that had pages of error signals and warnings. He explained that the systems of my computer were not working together properly; each time I used a new program, malfunctions were occurring. The problem wasn't my incompetence; it was the programming system. I was so relieved! We finally replaced the corrupted computer.

In the same way, because sin entered our world, the "programing systems" of our hearts have been corrupted (Jeremiah 17.9) But God has given us the Holy Spirit as our tech support and a brand-new heart through Jesus Christ. Because of Jesus' sacrifice on the cross, we literally become a new creation—the old life is gone and the new one begins (2 Corinthians 5.17). As we communicate with God, read the Bible, and grow in a local church, the Holy Spirit teaches us how to walk according to the systems of our new heart, and we begin to be transformed into the likeness of Christ (2 Corinthians 3.18).

There is something so freeing in knowing that though our hearts are indeed corrupted by sin, we have the awesome privilege of claiming a new heart in Christ! And though our old tainted heart systems try to regain control, the Holy Spirit will give us warning signals to remind us to rely only on His system of TRUTH. God also gives us lots of grace because He understands that we are trying to use our new perfected heart systems in a world still corrupted by sin. But we can have peace knowing that God has already given us the victory through Jesus!

"I will give you a new heart and put a new spirit in you; I will remove from you your heart of stone and give you a heart of flesh" (Ezekiel 36.26 NIV).

105

Bond Fruit

"For do I now persuade men, or God? Or do I seek to please men? For if I still pleased men, I would not be a bondservant of Christ" (Galatians 1.10 NKJV).

The surest way for us to completely miss out on God's purpose for our lives is to busy ourselves with distractions. Many times, God allows seasons of difficulty in our lives, which grow and mature us. These times may seem frustrating because we feel like they have nothing to do with our purpose; but if these struggles are ordained by God, they do have significance. However, I don't want to focus on the God-appointed circumstances in our lives; I want to talk about the flesh-appointed circumstances in our lives.

The Tree of Knowledge has two sides—Good and Evil. The fruit from this tree can be obviously bad, but it can also be deceptively good. It is very easy for us to pluck a fruit from this tree and consume it because in our minds we are achieving a good fruit or a "good work." But if that fruit is not rooted in God's heart and plan, it is evil no matter how tasty it seems.

Christians wear themselves thin because we are harvesting good fruit that is not part of our specifically designed destiny. We are serving idols that have replaced God's purposes in our lives. An idol is anything—good or bad—that consumes our devotion more than God. I believe the number one cause of this sin is due to the need to please others, not God.

We make decisions based on what will look good to people and what seems "appropriate" to us, instead of what the Holy Spirit is leading us to do. But I have learned from experience that what God has planned for our lives usually doesn't make sense until His glory fills our faith-choices and we finally see all the puzzle pieces fall into place. This takes time and we must wait!

Before we make any decisions or take any actions, we need to ask ourselves, "Is this fruit rooted in the Tree of Life?" Is our step based on faith in God or fear of others? Because if we aren't careful, our entire lives will be motivated by fear. But God's purpose in our lives will always be motivated by faith.

The fruit of bondage will leave us tired, frustrated and empty. The fruit of blessing will leave us satisfied, peaceful and filled with the Holy Spirit. Don't allow the enemy to tempt you with the seemingly "good" fruit of bondage. Satan will do anything to make you miss your purpose, because he knows that your God-centered destiny will have the power, authority and strength of Christ. Our goal should always be to please the Father—no matter what we and other people think.

"For this reason we also, since the day we heard it, do not cease to pray for you, and to ask that you may be filled with the knowledge of His will in all wisdom and spiritual understanding; that you may walk worthy of the Lord, fully pleasing Him, being fruitful in every good work and increasing in the knowledge of God; strengthened with all might, according to His glorious power, for all patience and longsuffering with joy; giving thanks to the Father who has qualified us to be partakers of the inheritance of the saints in the light" (Colossians 1.9-12 NKJV).

Never Give Up

Never giving up has been a hard lesson for me to learn. After years of standing on God's promises by faith, I understand how easy it would be to fold up my dreams and toss them into the nearest garbage pail of failure. Although my patience, endurance and resolve have improved, I have discovered the key factor that prevents me from throwing in the towel. This truth may seem simple and obvious, but I believe it is not aggressively sought after in the everyday, ins-and-outs of normal life. This choice has nothing to do with determination, strength or fortitude; and has everything to do with losing one's life in Christ.

The choice is submission.

I know that submission has many connotations, but I want to focus on the freedom found in not having our own agendas, timelines, plans, schedules, ideas and standards based on the extremely limited and dull imagination of the human mind compared to the mighty thoughts and plans of God. "For just as the heavens are higher than the earth, so my ways are higher than your ways and my thoughts higher than your thoughts" (Isaiah 55.9 NLT).

God's promises are so beautiful and so profound that we can't possibly fathom how they will come to life and what they will look like when they do. Submission allows us to remain content in the fruition of God's plan even when it doesn't line up with our expectations.

The dominating factor that urges me to quit is the feeling of disappointment. When I try to force my plans into God's will for my life, I will automatically be set up for major heartache because His ways are not my ways. I can look back at all the times I felt like God let me down, and they were each due to my own idea of how God's promises should be unfolding in my life. I have finally come to the conclusion that I will never be able to guess God's movement; and, unlike my plans, I am completely confident that His plans will benefit His Kingdom, Glorify His name and rescue His people from sin.

Therefore, I can shed the worry that comes with organizing my life according to my expectations, and I can rest in the knowledge that God can be trusted to fulfill His promises no matter what my circumstances look like, no matter what other people say and no matter what mistakes I make along the way. "Let us hold unswervingly to the hope we profess, for he who promised is faithful" (Hebrews 10.23 NIV).

God is faithful, and He uses His infinite imagination to fulfill His will in new and amazing ways. Instead of fighting, we should buckle up in this roller-coaster ride of life and hang on tightly to a God who loves us and wants us to have an eternal purpose.

"For I am about to do something new. See, I have already begun! Do you not see it? I will make a pathway through the wilderness. I will create rivers in the dry wasteland" (Isaiah 43.19 NLT).

Finding Rest in Autumn

Fall is my favorite season. I love crisp evening breezes filled with scents of pumpkin, spices and vanilla. I adore the palette of reds, browns, oranges and yellows across God's creation. I can't wait to forget the swimsuit in the drawer and pull out my knitted scarves, tailored jackets, boot-cut jeans and long-sleeve t-shirts.

I crave cool morning jogs, steaming cups of chai latte, bowls of homemade chili, naked tree branches, rolled down car windows and early sunsets.

I also look forward to the rest after harvest. And that's what fall symbolizes to me—the winding down of good work and the exhale after a job well done.

God calls us all to be workers for Christ in the fields of this world (Matthew 9.37-38). Often, we have seasons of intense dedication, discipline and determination. We stay balanced but busy sowing a harvest in God's Kingdom. We take the precious seeds that God has given us; and we use up all our strength, resources and energy planting every one. And when the time is right, we harvest the fruits of our labor and create offerings for the spiritually, emotionally, intellectually and physically hungry.

Finally, we wipe the sweat from our brow and note the chill in the air and the soft whisper from the Holy Spirit telling us it is now time to rest—not only to rest but to be the first to partake in the harvest. As Christians, we often emphasize the need to serve others, but we forget that the Bible demands that we enjoy the fruits of our labor as well: "The hardworking farmer must be first to partake of the crops" (2 Timothy 2.6 NKJV).

We shouldn't let guilt rob us of finding rest in God and enjoying the harvest we worked hard to produce. We grit our teeth and press on through the hard times, so we should laugh out loud and take a breather during the easy times. We must learn to rest, to graciously accept help and to say no when we feel God telling us to slow down. Part of a disciplined life is knowing when to find shelter in God and rejuvenate our spirits, minds, hearts and bodies in His presence.

"Nothing is better for a man than that he should eat and drink, and that his soul should enjoy good in his labor. This also, I saw, was from the hand of God" (Ecclesiastes 2.24 NKJV).

Face-to-Face

When I was a little girl, my maternal grandfather used to sit me on his lap in front of a mirror attached to a small desk in his living room. As we stared at each other's reflection, he would ask me questions that encouraged me to open up about myself.

"What age would you like to be?" he'd ask, while smiling at my image in the mirror.

"Sixteen," I answered, staring back at his aged reflection.

"Why sixteen?" he'd inquire with genuine interest.

"Because I can wear makeup and drive a car," I answered, trying my best to envision myself as a grownup.

My grandfather continued to ask me questions about my favorite colors and animals, and all the while I soaked up every detail of his face. I have many memories of my grandfather's rapid decline after his stroke, but my strongest image of him is when we chatted face to face in front of that living room mirror. I may not know much about him personally, but those short moments together have permanently imprinted themselves in my mind and heart.

I wonder, though, sometimes: what if we had a lifetime filled with intimate moments talking comfortably face-to-face? My grandfather was patient, and he knew I was young. He'd ask me very simple questions about my likes and dislikes. But what if we had continued talking as I grew in maturity, understanding and stature? What if our conversations had become less one-sided? What if I had started asking questions about him? Would we have been able to really get to know each other inside and out?

Although I never got the chance to continue my face-to-face chats with my grandfather, I am grateful and honored that I get these moments with my Creator. When I first started talking with God, our conversations paralleled my early chats with my grandfather. I constantly talked about my likes and dislikes. I envisioned all the wonderful things God had planned for my life. God was patient with me, and He encouraged me to get to know who I was, so I would eventually know who I was in Christ.

Over time, through prayer and reading God's Word, I began to see God's character take shape. I see what pleases Him, I see His hand at work and I see all the love He has for me. I don't have a physical image of Him, but slowly His nature is being imprinted in my mind and heart. I see His face in a song, over a difficultly, across the horizon, or on a friend's life. God moves through everything, and His thumbprint cannot be overlooked. I will spend eternity filling my eyes with His beauty.

My intimacy with God is growing. I may have a long way yet to go, but I know Him better than I did yesterday, last year, and ten years ago. I've learned not to pressure growth nor to neglect it; rather, I seek my God like I seek a familiar face. I talk with Him, I read His Word and I listen for His whisper. I still get it wrong, and my own desires clog up my ears and fog up my eyes; but God is always patient with me. He continues to initiate intimacy, and I make time to sit with Him—face to face.

"Jacob named the place Peniel (which means "face of God"), for he said, 'I have seen God face to face, yet my life has been spared'"

113

(Genesis 32.30 NLT).

Wield Your Ax

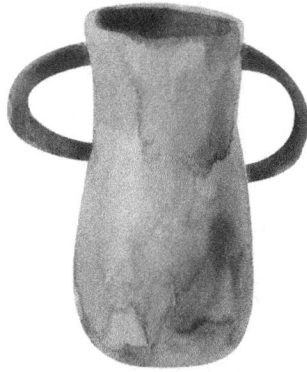

"The company of the prophets said to Elisha, 'Look, the place where we meet with you is too small for us. Let us go to the Jordan, where each of us can get a pole; and let us build a place there for us to meet.'"

"And he said, 'Go.'"

"Then one of them said, 'Won't you please come with your servants?'"

"'I will,' Elisha replied. And he went with them."

"They went to the Jordan and began to cut down trees. As one of them was cutting down a tree, the iron ax head fell into the water. 'Oh no, my lord!' he cried out. 'It was borrowed!'"

"The man of God asked, 'Where did it fall?' When he showed him the place, Elisha cut a stick and threw it there, and made the iron float. 'Lift it out,' he said. Then the man reached out his hand and took it."

People can get confused by this amazing miracle tucked in 2 Kings 6.1-7 (NIV). Some try to trivialize Elisha's actions for this unknown prophet who dropped his ax. But God does not waste a single aspect of His Word to coincidence, entertainment or frivolity. Everything in the Old and the New Testaments points to Jesus; and when we read over the Scriptures with this understanding, we will have a better and fuller understanding of our Messiah.

And since we, as Born-Again Believers, have died and were raised to life in Christ (Romans 6.4); we also gain a better understanding of who we are in Jesus and of our role in His Kingdom Plan. For when every passage speaks of Jesus, we can see ourselves tucked in the middle of Him.

"I pray that they will all be one, just as you and I are one—as you are in me, Father, and I am in you. And may they be in us so that the world will believe you sent me" (John 17.21 NLT).

The prophets realize that their capacity has grown larger than their territory, so they feel led to begin the process of expanding their land. Has your ability outgrown your territory? Do you have a God-given desire to expand?

After the prophets get Elisha's approval to expand, they ask for Elisha (symbolic of Jesus) to go with them. Have you asked God for His anointing? Is Jesus in the center of your growth, change and movement?

The prophets all begin their work, but the "chosen" prophet's iron ax falls into the Jordan. Has your dream been sunk? Has your vision died? Are you at a dead end and in need of a miracle?

The ax is made of iron (symbolic of strength). Have you seen all of your hard work disappear without a harvest? Are you wondering if you have great faith or if you are just a fool?

The ax is borrowed, which causes the chosen prophet to cry out. Do you realize that your gifts and talents are borrowed from the Master for a limited time? Have you placed great value over all that God has given you stewardship?

Instead of diving into the water to search for the ax, the chosen prophet

116

asks Elisha to help him. Do you realize that your dream must die, so it can be resurrected in God's power? Did you know that your efforts to save your dream only slap away God's mighty hand?

The chosen prophet shows Elisha where the ax has fallen. Have you stayed focused on the vision that God has placed in your heart? Have you kept your eyes on your dream even though you can no longer physically see it?

Elisha threw the stick (symbolic of humanity) into the water. Did you know that Jesus is the branch (Isaiah 11.1)? Did you know that Jesus' humanity released God's resurrection power on this earth (Ephesians 1.18-20)? Did you know that this power lives in you and can resurrect your dream (Romans 8.11 and John 14.13)?

Elisha told the chosen prophet to grab hold of the ax and lift it out of the water....

When God brings your vision back to life, do not wait. Reach out and take hold of your promises and use them to give God all the glory. You have worked hard; you have believed against all odds. You have waited with your eyes on Christ while your vision transformed in the tomb. You have been chosen and separated for this purpose. Your strength is now aligned with the Holy Spirit.

Do not squander what Jesus died to give you. The water has anointed your hand and your work. Take hold of your ax and claim the Promised Land that God has prepared for you. Use your ax until there is nothing left, and Jesus will look at you from the gates of heaven and say, "Well done, my good and faithful servant. You have been faithful in handling this small amount, so now I will give you many more responsibilities. Let's celebrate together!" (Matthew 25.23 NLT).

Drawn to Eternity

When I was a little girl in Kansas, a tornado came through my neighborhood. I ran home with my feet barely touching the ground as the wind tried to suck me to its center. When I finally made it to our front door, my mom reached out her hand and pulled me into our house. My body flew horizontally, and I dove into the entryway like a bird. I'll never forget the day that I walked the earth with a constant pull of nature drawing me away from my reality.

As we walk the path of our existence, I wonder if our spirits are not continuously drawn toward eternity. We wear our flesh, think with our minds and live through our souls (personalities), but our spirits are not temporal. We were created in God who is everlasting. Though we have a starting point at Creation (unlike God who has always been), we do not have an ending point (John 3.16)—we continue after these bodies die and this world wears out (Isaiah 51.6). We will be given new bodies and a New Earth (Revelation 21.1 & Philippians 3.21). We walk into our real Promised Land and live out our true purpose in heaven.

As I live the quickly turning pages in the current chapter of my life, I battle the pull of God's gravity toward what is real. I know this temporary life has purpose, and I appreciate all that God is doing, but I have a strong sense that this is only a shadow or a whisper of what's to come (Psalm 144.4). God is so imaginative and so awesome that He doesn't waste one second of my life to indifferent coincidence. When I look closely, God is weaving the details of all existence into an eternal picture that overshadows the physical world. But I notice that I often distract myself from watching the beautiful story unfold because perhaps I fear the full knowledge of my displacement.

How did Jesus handle it? He has no starting point: He is the Alpha and Omega (Revelation 22.13). He gave up His glory (Philippians 2.7 & John 17.5), became flesh (John 1.14) and took our sins (1 Peter 2.24), so that we could live our eternal existence in the amazing presence of our Creator. How could He live in a world corrupted by sin knowing His perfect home and throne were waiting for Him just over the physical horizon? Everything in Him was drawn to the Father, yet He rooted His feet on this earth because of His intense love for us, His beloved creation.

I wonder if Jesus slipped away to solitary places so often because He too was homesick. When the longing for home intensified, He prayed to His Father and found refreshment in His spirit. I think that many times when we get homesick, we try to distract ourselves with things that don't sedate our desire for heaven. We'll waste hours upon hours on trivial things, hoping that our homesickness fades. But the time, money and energy we've used up only leave us empty.

I'm determined that when my spirit becomes restless that instead of desperately diverting my attention from what's really bothering me, I can go to the Father and have Him fill me with His peace, purpose and presence. My spirit longs for God. His presence is what continually draws me to eternity. Jesus' sacrifice on the cross enabled the Holy Spirit to dwell inside of me. If I would simply slip away to spend time with Him every day, I wouldn't be homesick because God is my home.

"For we know that when this earthly tent we live in is taken down (that is, when we die and leave this earthly body), we will have a house in heaven, an eternal body made for us by God himself and not by human hands. We grow weary in our present bodies, and we long to put on our heavenly bodies like new clothing. For we will put on heavenly bodies; we will not be spirits without bodies. While we live in these earthly bodies, we groan and sigh, but it's not that we want to die and get rid of these bodies that clothe us. Rather, we want to put on our new bodies so that these dying bodies will be swallowed up by life. God himself has prepared us for this, and as a guarantee he has given us his Holy Spirit" (2 Corinthians 5.1-5 NLT).

Waiting in Saturday

You can feel those moments when God is calling you to a significant opportunity of sacrifice. There's usually a huge internal struggle because a war that you can't see is being fought for your destiny (Ephesians 6.10-20). The enemy has been on this earth a long time, and he has dealt with many people; he knows what it takes to stop you from walking into God's promises (1 Peter 5.8).

You are faced with a choice: You can sow the seed of faith or a hide it away out of fear, indifference or selfishness.

Jesus experienced this struggle before He sowed the seed of His sacrifice for the sins of all mankind. His internal battle was great: "Then he [Jesus] said to them, 'My soul is overwhelmed with sorrow to the point of death. Stay here and keep watch with me'" (Matthew 26.38 NIV).

Even though Jesus' sole purpose was to be our Redeemer, He begged God to take that portion of His destiny away: "Going a little farther, he fell with his face to the ground and prayed, 'My Father, if it is possible, may this cup be taken from me. Yet not as I will, but as you will'" (Matthew 26.39 NIV). If Jesus resisted fulfilling His purpose, you better believe you will too.

But what if you sow that seed of faith? What if you deny the will of your flesh and follow God's leading into sacrifice? What happens when you are done? Do you see the fruit right away? Do you experience the resurrection of life that God has promised you immediately? Do you dance to a victory song through the streets of town only moments after the seed has been planted?

Probably not.

Jesus died on the cross for our sins on a Friday, but He didn't resurrect in all His glory until Sunday. So what was happening on Saturday?

Saturday is imperative to a faith seed that has been sown. Once a seed is planted, it must die before new life begins to grow. This transference of life takes time, especially if the faith seed is a big one. You might not see anything happening, and you may be tempted to lose hope or give up. But don't. Your sacrifice is not wasted! Your seed will be resurrected!

Trust that God will fulfill His promises to you. Believe that "new life" is springing up in the spiritual realm and will manifest before your eyes soon. Don't lose courage; don't lose heart. Keep holding onto your faith that God will come through for you! And when you're surrounded by God's bountiful harvest, sow more seeds of faith and share with everyone what He has done!

"Timing is so important! If you are going to be successful in dance, you must be able to respond to rhythm and timing. It's the same in the Spirit. People who don't understand God's timing can become spiritually spastic, trying to make the right things happen at the wrong time. They don't get His rhythm – and everyone can tell they are out of step. They birth things prematurely, threatening the very lives of their God-given dreams." – T. D. Jakes

Doing What it Takes

"And he [the King] said to his servants, 'The wedding feast is ready, and the guests I invited aren't worthy of the honor. Now go out to the street corners and invite everyone you see.' So the servants brought in everyone they could find, good and bad alike, and the banquet hall was filled with guests" (Matthew 22.8-10 NLT).

It had been about ten months since my last hair appointment, so I scheduled a trim with layers about an hour before my date night with my husband. I felt particularly clever because I didn't have to fix my hair for the date. I walked into the salon with the same ponytail I wore to my morning workout and walked out with beautifully styled hair!

The young lady who styled my hair was super sweet, and my radar was on for any opening to talk about Christ, church or the Bible. I try to follow the Holy Spirit's lead when opening up about my relationship with God because one word can totally turn someone away from the Christ I'm presenting. I know that I've got to reach people where they're at, not where I'm at.

I asked the young lady many questions, genuinely interested in her life and design. I revealed a lot about myself and tried to encourage her with any wisdom I thought might apply to her life. I found out that she was single, and I could tell she really wanted to meet a nice guy. And there it was—my tiny drop of a lead into the all-encompassing ocean of Christ!

"Did you know that my church is the biggest meeting place for singles in the city?" I asked.

"Really! Wow, I need to go to your church! Where do you go?" she asked.

And there I had it: A tiny gateway into God.

Now, I know that this doesn't sound super spiritual, but what if she goes to church looking for a man and finds Jesus? What I've learned is that God fills me with His wisdom, so the Holy Spirit can pick and choose what I say depending on WHO I'm talking to. At first, God may use people's selfishness to bring them into relationship with Him; but as they become stronger in their faith, He will begin to use their sacrifice to draw them into His likeness.

Jesus describes the Kingdom of God like a wedding feast in Matthew 22, and the King sent His servants out to invite EVERYONE they could find! I am one of the King's servants, and I need to use every tactic I have in my arsenal to get people into the Kingdom of God. I must do my best to size up each person and entice him/her to join the feast with anything that piques his/her interest. As long as I stay under the authority of the Holy Spirit and the Bible, I can do whatever it takes to fill God's banquet halls.

"They are serving the best food at this banquet! You don't want to miss this dinner!"

"There will be some pretty famous people at this banquet! You need to see what they are wearing!"

"They are giving away gold at this banquet! You could buy yourself a new coat!"

"There are so many intellects at this banquet! You'll rub elbows with the greatest minds of our day!"

"The King of this banquet is totally awesome! He'll make you feel like a thousand bucks!"

"People are getting healed at this banquet! You can find relief from your pain!"

"There is going to be some crazy entertainment at this banquet! You'll love the music!"

"The Creator of the Universe is hosting this banquet! He'll tell you what life is truly about!"

The servants' sole purpose was to use their God-given passions to creatively find ways to bring people to the feast where they will meet the King face-to-face. Since the King sent out many different servants, they will each reach people in distinct and unique ways. The King gave all the servants a specific vision, so they could find and influence a certain population of people to celebrate the union of Christ and the Church in the banquet halls of heaven for eternity!

What irritates me most about this principle of reaching the lost is when the King's servants start ridiculing each other about their methods of bringing people to the feast. I've read many books written by a wide range of Christian leaders, and they all have a heart to reach people. However, they all have their own reaching-the-lost vision because God has a certain group of people He specifically wants them to invite. We confuse potential wedding guests when we fight over different methods of getting them to the King's table.

So before we judge a person's or a ministry's vision of how to reach the lost, we should look at their fruit. Are they bringing people to the feast? Are people meeting the King face-to-face? Are people entering the feast by the only door, Christ? We might not understand their methods or relate to the people they are reaching, but we can certainly cheer them on! When God's people put aside their differences and unite for the cause of Christ, the world will have no choice but to listen to the Good News that we are preaching.

"Even though I am a free man with no master, I have become a slave to all people to bring many to Christ. When I was with the Jews, I lived like a Jew to bring the Jews to Christ. When I was with those who follow the Jewish law, I too lived under that law. Even though I am not subject to the law, I did this so I could bring to Christ those who are under the law. When I am with the Gentiles who do not follow the Jewish law, I too live apart from that law so I can bring them to Christ. But I do not ignore the law of God; I obey the law of Christ. When I am with those who are weak, I share their weakness, for I want to bring the weak to Christ. Yes, I try to find common ground with everyone, doing everything I can to save some. I do everything to spread the Good News and share in its blessings" (1 Corinthians 9.19-23 NLT).

Ridiculous Belief

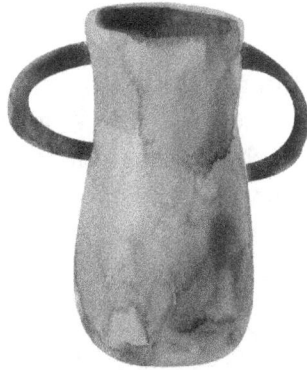

God called Moses to tell Pharaoh to release the Israelites from slavery (Exodus 3.8). This demand is borderline ludicrous because the entire infrastructure of Egyptian economic and social systems during this time pivot on having free labor. Allowing the Hebrew people to just walk away from the Egyptian nation would be like prohibiting the use of fuel, electricity and all other forms of power in the United States.

Cars – gone. Dishwashers – gone. Air conditioning – gone. Internet – gone.

Cell phones, stop lights, power tools, microwaves, blow dryers, sewing machines, social media, refrigerators, medical equipment… all disappear overnight. The American culture as we know it would collapse, and we would have to scramble to find our new footing in a world without mass sources of energy.

No wonder Moses felt just a touch intimidated about telling Pharaoh to let his mass source of energy (the Hebrew people) go. What I find interesting, though, is that Moses never questions the probability of God's plan; he merely questions the adequacy of his own ability.

Several times Moses tells God that the Hebrew people and Pharaoh won't listen to him because he's not a good speaker (Exodus 4.10, 6.12

& 6.30). In fact, Moses pleads for God to send someone else (Exodus 4.13). But Moses doesn't tell God that he thinks the whole situation is impossible because he knows that with God ALL things are possible (Matt 19.26).

God could help Moses through his low self-image and his weaknesses, but Moses had to have belief in God's Word first. Pharaoh might not have believed, and the Hebrews might not have believed, but Moses believed. And His faith is what sets him apart.

Christians who are set apart are not necessarily eloquent, confident or brilliant; rather, they believe God's promises. They believe God even when the rest of the world doesn't. They believe God even when the promises seem ridiculously impossible.

This truth should give us peace. When we realize that it's not about our performance but about His faithfulness, we can rest assure that God will fulfill what He says. We will never be perfect as we walk in faith, but God will provide us with help along the way.

"But Moses protested to God, 'Who am I to appear before Pharaoh? Who am I to lead the people of Israel out of Egypt?'" (Exodus 3.11 NLT).

Falling Asleep at the Wheel

When I was 10 years old, I got really good at riding my bike. In fact, I was so proficient that I wouldn't use my hands to steer. I'd let my arms dangle by my side and use my body to balance. I remember one beautiful, sunny afternoon I was leisurely riding my bike around my neighborhood. A wonderfully long stretch of road extended right in front of my cul-de-sac, and I enjoyed taking a rest on my bike as gravity pulled me down the gentle descent.

With the sun hitting my face and the breeze blowing through my hair, I decided to close my eyes. I woke up several hours later on my couch. Bruises, scrapes and grass stains covered my body. I had fallen asleep at the wheel and crashed onto a small, thin patch of grass on the curbside. As I tried to pull my aching body up, I wondered how anyone could take a nap while riding a bike.

Now, as an adult, I can see how easy it is to "fall asleep at the wheel" of our lives. We become over-confident in our faith, relationships and responsibilities; and we allow gravity to pull our valuable seconds into aimless stagnation. We are tempted to close our eyes and slowly let the zeal for our God, spouse, children, friends, health, church and purpose fall asleep.

I understand that God gives us much needed seasons of rest; but even in our respite, we can maintain a godly awareness of God's Kingdom coming to fulfillment around us. We are called to be good stewards of the amazing people, possessions and passions He has given us; and we are to use our God-given free will to promote God's best in all aspects of life. Each day and every decision no matter how mundane or how small contains great significance and purpose. God's wisdom and favor encompass the singleness of one breath and the scope of all our breaths combined.

The fact remains that we will never be as proficient in life as Jesus. Jesus is perfect, and we can maintain a hunger for His likeness that is seasoned with grace and drenched in love. If we strive to achieve an honest perspective of our strengths and weaknesses, we'll be able to rejoice in how far we've come while staying focused on where we need to go. There is immense joy in knowing that we still have much to learn, room to grow and time to change. Our lives aren't complete until we see Jesus face to face; so until then, we need to keep our eyes on Him and our hearts on eternity.

"I don't mean to say that I have already achieved these things or that I have already reached perfection. But I press on to possess that perfection for which Christ Jesus first possessed me. No, dear brothers and sisters, I have not achieved it, but I focus on this one thing: Forgetting the past and looking forward to what lies ahead" (Philippians 3.12-13 NLT).

The Walking

I began reading the Bible fresh for the New Year. I dove into God's perfect creation and His gift of free will to His beloved people made in His image. I saw humanity's embrace of sin and the consequent corruption of God's perfect design. After Cain killed his brother, Abel; Eve gave birth to Seth, the son of redemption. Seth began his family, and the Bible then reads something that I thought interesting: "And as for Seth, to him also a son was born; and he named him Enosh. Then men began to call on the name of the LORD" (Genesis 4.26 NKJV).

This verse struck me because the wickedness and judgment of people is quickly covered in the subsequent chapters. If people were calling on the name of the Lord, why did God cause a flood to erase almost the entire population from the face of the earth? How did Noah find favor and grace with God to be the seed of God's redemption plan for humanity?

Finally, I read four little words and found my answer: "Noah walked with God" (Genesis 6.9 NKJV).

I've come to the conclusion that many people call on the name of the Lord, but very few people make it a priority to walk with the Lord on a daily basis. I know this because I used to be one of them. I loved God with my words, my hopes and my intentions; but my thoughts, actions and decisions over the long haul revealed that He had very little hold over my heart. I wanted to love God from a distance because I was scared to let Him into the crevices of my life. If I loved God with all my strength, mind and soul; I would have to give Him complete control and confront my own selfish nature.

Intimacy with God ignites the most romantic, heartbreaking, fierce, loving, tumultuous, exasperating, fulfilling, difficult, revealing, joyous relationship that even the best films in Hollywood couldn't capture. Walking with God is not always easy. Yes, it is beautiful, exciting and rewarding. Nevertheless, it takes a lot of faith, trust, sacrifice and obedience. Merely calling on the name of the Lord would be so much easier because it can be dictated by our standards, timetable and needs. However, calling on God without really walking with Him would eventually lead to our stagnation, idolatry and ruin.

So as I walk with God, I'm reminded that like any relationship there are seasons of pressing, refining and breaking; but there are also seasons of growth, renewal and victory. And the one thing that I've learned that makes my load lighter and the yoke of faith with Christ easier to bear is that it's not about who I am, but about who He is. And He is perfect in every way, and that truth gives me peace, hope and joy. If I could just tuck myself into His grace and remain in the fold of His love, I would find the strength to walk with Him to the ends of the earth and back.

"If we only have the will to walk, then God is pleased with our stumbles." - C.S. Lewis

The Christmas Yearbook

"For God so loved the world that he gave his one and only Son, that whoever believes in him shall not perish but have eternal life" (John 3.16 NIV).

When I was a junior in high school, we had a spirit week that led up to homecoming. During this week, every day was a fun dress-up day. On mismatch day, I went all out. I wore the tackiest, most uncoordinated outfit that I could imagine. It actually felt quite liberating not to fuss over whether my ensemble was fashionable, put-together or even well received. I was unrestrained by high school trend-setting rules, and I walked through the halls without worrying of whether everything was tucked in and set properly.

The coolest part of my day happened in fifth period. One of the girls from yearbook came to our classroom looking to take photos of a good mismatch outfit. She took one look at me, and asked if I would come out in the hallway for a photo op. Of course, I jumped out of my seat lickety-split and headed to the door. Since it was mismatch day, I gave her my craziest pose—hands up in the air, head tilted to the side and mouth formed into a wide, goofy smile. I walked back to my seat knowing that my photo would be an awesome tribute to spirit week and mismatch day.

The following semester when the yearbook came out, I couldn't wait to see if my photo made it into print. I instantly flipped through the pages of the large book, looking for my much-anticipated mismatch day tribute. When I finally found it, I was shocked! My photo was everything I wanted. It was wild, fun and uncoordinated. However, the only problem was that there was absolutely no mention of mismatch day. In fact, the caption listed my name and that I was showing off my particular, crazy style sense. WHAT?

The photo now took on an entirely new meaning that had little to do with the realities of mismatch day and the legitimacy of my weird wardrobe. The photo was taken completely out of context and reconstructed within an alternate motive (aka my individual and crazy sense of style). I'm sure the photo was selected with mismatch day long forgotten, and the yearbook students were simply trying to capture a unique story; but I still found the departure from the initial intent to be misleading.

If Christmas were a yearbook, it would be filled with many such mismatch stories. Our culture today produces a plethora of unique variations of the Christmas holiday, but sadly most of them have been taken completely out of context and reconstructed within an alternate motive. The true meaning of Christmas is quickly being forgotten, and individuals flip through the pages of today's Christmas Yearbook intrigued, entertained and confused by all the variations of single a reality.

Laying aside the countless Santas and reindeer; winter songs and cups of cocoa; wrapped presents and twinkling lights; holiday cards and donation boxes; Christmas is about a perfect God becoming flesh to save a creation separated by sin. God created a flawless world and a flawless people, but He gave us free will to choose His perfection (Tree of Life) or our own corruption (Tree of Knowledge of Good and Evil). We chose to leave God's righteousness, so sin penetrated our world, corrupting the earth and the hearts of people. Our sin formed a chasm between fallen humanity and their perfect Creator.

God knew we would fall short of His holiness, but instead of disregarding us altogether, He created a redemption plan: He would set aside His glory, enter our corrupted world and exchange His righteousness for our sins. The Creator of the Universe chose the name Jesus and took our mistakes, ugliness and guilt because He loves us that much. He became a helpless baby in a manger, so we could have a personal relationship with Him.

Our time on this earth is short; and every Christmas season that goes by, I am reminded that I have life because Jesus chose death. I have eternity in heaven with a perfect God because Jesus' pierced hands have closed the gap that separates me from Him. In the middle of my Christmas Yearbook—on the only page that gives me hope, joy and Truth—I see my God, salvation wrapped in flesh, and I'm in awe of the greatest gift the world has ever seen: Jesus, called Immanuel, God is with us.

"The virgin will be with child and will give birth to a son, and they will call him Immanuel"—which means, 'God with us'" (Matthew 1.23 NIV).

Proud to be a Slug

Question: "Comparing different slug groups arises quickly the question, how those shell-less snails could survive, without the protection of a shell."

Answer: "The external protection of a slug mainly happens by its mucus or slime."

I've been telling God lately that being obedient to Him is making me feel like a snail without a shell. A shell-less snail is called a slug, so I guess I feel like a slug. I've been on my slug-journey for about four years now. My self-esteem used to be connected to a lot of things (fitness, education, accomplishments, money, etc.), but God has slowly cut everything until all I have left is Him.

This doesn't mean He has actually taken everything from me, but He has taken my dependency on everything. I can survive if I lose everything, but I cannot survive if I lose God. Without God there is absolute nothingness—no beauty, no education, no accomplishments, no money, no family, no anything! Without God I wouldn't be typing this in my laptop at the coffee house, and you wouldn't be reading this from your computer at work or home. We wouldn't exist.

If we live the slug-life by putting God first, we gain everything in the process (Matthew 6.33). But putting God first is not easy. Putting God first means allowing God to take our snail shells (our efforts at self-glory) off. Without our snail shells, we are vulnerable and exposed to the world, which is exactly what God wants. It is only when our snail shells are off that Jesus' light that He planted in each of us can shine in this dark world (John 8.12).

But what does the slug life look like? You can see it when you examine Jesus' life.

If you read Isaiah's foreshadowing of Jesus, you get an image of a very ordinary man (Isaiah 53.2-5 NIV). Jesus was God in the flesh, yet the Scriptures describe Him in very humble terms: "He had no beauty or majesty to attract us to him, nothing in his appearance that we should desire him. He was despised and rejected by men, a man of sorrows, and familiar with suffering" (2-3). This was Jesus' humanity. Not so very pretty (I hate saying that, but it is a biblical fact).

However, if you read Daniel's description of Jesus, you get an entirely different image (Daniel 10.4-8 NIV). This description of Jesus boasts a super-natural and awe-inspiring image: "His body was like chrysolite, his face like lightning, his eyes like flaming torches, his arms and legs like the gleam of burnished bronze, and his voice like the sound of a multitude" (6). This is an image of the Son of God, the King of the Jews! When Daniel saw this Jesus, he said, "I had no strength left, my face turned deathly pale and I was helpless" (8).

Jesus took off His snail shell (His perfect glory) and humbled Himself to the world. He allowed us to mock Him, persecute Him and kill Him. At any moment, He could put on His snail shell, but He didn't. Why Did Jesus allow Himself to be despised and not worshiped? God had a plan:

"When he sees all that is accomplished by his anguish, he will be satisfied. And because of his experience, my righteous servant will make it possible for many to be counted righteous, for he will bear all their sins" (Isaiah 53.11 NLT).

Jesus humbled Himself so that we may gain righteousness (right-standing with God) through His sacrifice for our sins.

What does that mean for you and me? It means this: If Jesus took off His snail shell which was perfect, why do we have such a hard time taking ours off which is flawed by sin? Instead of humbling ourselves to this world, we pump-up our snail shells. We decorate our shells with degrees, clothes, cars, houses, achievements, beauty and pride. We lug around our bulging shells and knock over anyone in our way. How can we serve and love others if we are too busy bowling them over with our pride?

I'm not saying there is anything wrong with these things. But when we base our self-esteem on things of this world, we will be severely disappointed in the end. We can only find our self-esteem in the fact that we are created by the Most High God, and He loves us and has great plans for us. Once we fully understand that privilege, it won't be so difficult to take off our snail shells and humble ourselves.

But . . .

You say, "People constantly hurt me, and I need to defend myself!"

God says, "I was oppressed and afflicted, yet I did not defend myself."

You say, "People look down on me; they think I am nothing!"

God says, "I was despised and rejected; people hid their faces from me."

You say, "People accuse me of wrongs that I did not do!"

God says, "I was oppressed and judged, though, I never sinned."

How do we willingly humble ourselves to a world that will hurt us? If we take off our snail shells and become slugs, we'll be surrounded by a bunch of tough snails. Mostly everyone else is wearing their shells, and we're going to get bumped on and rolled over. How do we protect ourselves?

The answer is in the slime! The Holy Spirit is often symbolized as oil. King David was anointed with oil to represent that the Holy Spirit would be flowing through him. If we take our snail shells off and humble ourselves, we will be protected by an oily slime—the Holy Spirit!

Just imagine that when you are allowing the Holy Spirit to have complete control of your life, you're allowing your slug to be smothered with glistening slime. This slime will help whenever the other snail shells hit you. They'll try to take you out, but their efforts will just slide right off (2 Corinthians 4.8-9).

On the other hand, when you come into contact with other slugs, you'll have a holy slime swap! Their Holy Spirit will mix with your Holy Spirit, and your understanding of how wonderful God is will deepen. Our points of view are so limited, and that is why it is so important we surround ourselves with other Spirit-led people. If we can see God through the eyes of many righteous people, how awesome would our image of God be? But you've got to take off your shell first!

You say: "I'm a slug, God!"

God says: "…[I] chose the foolish things of the world to shame the wise; I chose the weak things of the world to shame the strong" (1 Corinthians 1.27 NIV).

God Confidence

I've always struggled with self-confidence. For much of my life, I allowed the enemy's arrows to strike through the heart of my self-worth and value. I thought I had to prove myself. I needed to be fit, smart, well liked, productive and esteemed. When something in my life wasn't going right, I would crumble into a big, mushy pile of insecurities. I would take my failings and wear them, unable to live in victory in any other areas of my life.

I couldn't be a good example of a righteous child of God because I allowed my feelings to dictate who I was in Christ. I was like a ship on the waves, going back and forth depending on the external forces. Who in their right mind would want to emulate my insecurity-driven life? Shouldn't Christians be brimming with confidence and worth because of the cross?

Finally, God brought me to a place in my life where He cut everything that I tied my self-worth and confidence to. I wallowed in my self-defeat until I looked to God for help. I realized that I placed very little value on the fact that I am a child of God and placed great value in what the world deemed as worthy. God showed me that when I form roots of self-worth to areas other than Him, they become idols and distract me from loving Him most.

God helped me cultivate a single, strong root to Him. He became my self-worth and confidence. I am the daughter of the Most High God, and He places great value and worth into me. I don't need to prove my worth because Christ proved it on the cross. God has chosen me for a special purpose, and He provides me lots of grace to accomplish His will.

Now when the waves of this life knock me around, I don't fall down in despair. I stand firm in God's promises, and I claim unseen victory. I don't bow down to the enemy's accusations. I only bow down to my Creator. All of my self-worth and confidence are wrapped up in Christ. I fear little else other than to lose His favor, His blessing, His smile. I no longer care about self-confidence or self-worth. All I want is God-confidence and God-worth.

"Or, you may fall on your knees and pray—to God's delight! You'll see God's smile and celebrate, finding yourself set right with God. You'll sing God's praises to everyone you meet, testifying, 'I messed up my life—and let me tell you, it wasn't worth it. But God stepped in and saved me from certain death. I'm alive again! Once more I see the light!'" (Job 33.26-28 MSG).

The Model Life

"And we know that the Son of God has come and has given us understanding, so that we may know him who is true; and we are in him who is true, in his Son Jesus Christ. He is the true God and eternal life" (1 John 5.20 ESV).

During graduate school, I worked as a leasing agent for an elegant residential apartment community. I was required to wear a three-piece suit in order to match the upscale vibe of the complex. Each unit had luxurious accents and features, and the exquisitely designed landscape and leasing office made working there very enjoyable.

One of my duties as the leasing agent was to prepare the model units. I'd show these units to prospective renters as examples of how the homes could look when they were occupied. Perfectly chosen furniture pieces and décor adorned each unit. There were no piles of bills, dishes, laundry or homework to be seen. No computer or television occupied any space. Only a small radio that played continuous soft contemporary music rested on a corner table.

Every morning, I looked forward to entering my perfect model homes. I'd turn on all the lights, switch the ceiling fans to medium for a perfect breeze, open all the curtains and spray floral potpourri in the air. My eyes would lovingly glide over the ensemble of furnishings, and my imagination would begin to create a perfect life. No research essays to write. No bills to pay. No dishes to clean. No bed to make. No looming responsibility to be done. I could just grab one of the classic books from the coffee table, sit back and indulge in endless free time.

After months and months of coveting one particular tropically decorated home, I finally indulged. I adored the master bedroom with its large, stylish bed that was always made. I would look at the thick, expensive comforter and wonder what it would feel like just to slip under the covers and close my eyes. I could dream away all the bills to be paid, all the chores to be done, all the homework to be finished and all the parts of life that I didn't like. I could finally merge myself into the perfect world of my model home.

At last, I turned down the bed, jumped under the sheets, tucked myself in and closed my eyes. My smile only lasted a few seconds until I caught wind of the stale layer of dust all around me. The bed itself did not have a mattress, and my bones jabbed into the hard box spring under me. I felt out of place, like I was stealing another person's nap. As hard as I tried, I couldn't get over the fact that I didn't belong. I quickly jumped out of the bed, looked around to make sure no one had seen my impulsive action and put the comforter back in its place.

Now I saw the model home with new eyes. Everything was fake. There were no clothes in the drawers, no food in the refrigerator, no soap in the bathroom and no pulse of life in the air. Though the model home looked perfect on the outside, it was lifeless, empty and joyless inside. The model home was a lie. No occupied unit that I had ever entered looked so clean and put together. All the beauty and romance I had developed for that home was washed away with one truth: Life is messy.

The movement of life is chaotic, imperfect and many times hectic, but it's also filled with emotion, truth and energy. I think many times we covet an ideal, seamless existence, but that doesn't exist. Jesus led a perfect life, but that doesn't mean His life wasn't messy. He offended, confused and disappointed people. Jesus talked to sinners, which offended people. He spoke in parables, which confused people. And He came as a lowly carpenter, which disappointed people. Jesus lived perfectly before God, but His life was often crazy, hectic and difficult.

Life is messy, but it is the mess that signifies life. I think once we fix our perspectives and realize that the model life we're groping for is only a fantasy, we'll be more content with the life (chaos, imperfections and mess) that we've been given. When we find satisfaction in our fabulously imperfect lives, we will begin to see all the beauty and blessings that surround us.

Every dish that we clean means that we broke bread with someone. Every load of laundry that we wash means we have a reason to dress up. Every assignment or project we complete means we are learning and growing. Every bed that we make means we got to live another day. We should be thankful for every mess because they signify that we have been given life!

"Without oxen a stable stays clean, but you need a strong ox for a large harvest" (Proverbs 14.4 NLT).

Roundhouse Kick

I recently injured the Achilles tendon in my left leg. I was doing roundhouse kicks with my right foot into a punching bag. I concentrated so much on my right leg, trying to make sure I didn't bruise or hurt it, that I didn't even notice that my left foot was under strain. I woke up the following morning and my left Achilles tendon was throbbing. I had no idea what had happened until I remembered the kicks from the day before.

I couldn't believe it! The bruises on my right leg from all the kicking had no effect on my ability to continue working out. But the tension I put on my left foot, forcing it to pivot and stabilize my vigorously moving body, prevented me from working out and even walking correctly. In fact, I had to wear an ankle wrap for several days and soak my entire leg several times in freezing water. I was so focused on my right leg that I totally missed the burden I placed on my left leg.

As I soaked my aching foot, I realized that I have done this in my relationships too. I've leaned on people to the point of strain, while I kept my focus on some seemingly important aspect of my life. I was so worried about getting bruised in a certain area that I didn't see the burden I was placing on others—a burden they should never be expected to carry.

It's easy to get so self-focused that we quit concentrating on the needs and feelings of those around us. Something big or crazy enters our world, and we expect people to be our pivot point and stability. Little do we know, however, that these people have worries and troubles of their own, and our extra weight causes them to buckle under the pressure and become wounded. We are shocked by their snap reaction, but our self-absorbed ignorance never once perceived the strain that we caused them.

People have their limits. They can only absorb so much pressure. But God is all-encompassing, and He can carry the weight of the world on His shoulders. Jesus says that if we yoke ourselves to Him, our burdens will be light and easy to carry (Matthew 11.30). We give Him our worries and needs, and He gives us back a peace that eases all of the stress and tension in our lives. This truth is a supernatural phenomenon, and it is available to us at any moment. Instead of putting our strain on others, we can put our trust in God who is able to take care of all our needs.

"Don't worry about anything; instead, pray about everything. Tell God what you need, and thank him for all he has done" (Philippians 4.6 NLT).

Record Player Passion

When I was a little girl, I used to sneak behind the couch and watch my father listen to his vinyl records. I could see my dad's military demeanor fade as the guitar and drums peeled out from the diamond-tipped phonograph needle. I couldn't understand the lyrics and I didn't quite grasp the power of music, but my young mind comprehended the excitement and passion my father had for Classic Rock. He loved it!

The memories I have of my father listening to music have always resonated with me. Every time I hear a Styx or Journey song, I'm connected back to my childhood. But the music didn't leave the impression on me; my dad's response to the music did. The joy I saw in my father's face caused Classic Rock to be a sweet spot in my life.

Many times as a Christian, I feel like I need to have all the answers. I seek understanding so that others can come to me and find some clarity. I wrestle with eternal questions—Why are we here? Why did God create life? Why do our eternal spirits dwell in dying bodies? I can't live out my days in peace unless I know there is a larger picture to creation than my short, little life. I desire to understand the character of God, the sacrifice of Christ, the movement of the Holy Spirit and how my purpose fits into eternity.

However, I believe my answers do not have the biggest impact on people—my passion does. People are looking to Christians. They want to see the joy that I saw in my father's face when he listened to music. They want to see our response to the "Good News." Are we passionate about our God? Are we overjoyed to know Christ more? Does the Holy Spirit shine through our day-to-day lives? Our response will have a greater impact than our answers ever will.

"And my speech and my message were not in plausible words of wisdom, but in demonstration of the Spirit and of power, that your faith might not rest in the wisdom of men but in the power of God" (1 Corinthians 2.4-5 ESV).

Paul wrote to the Church of Corinth that he didn't want his words about the Gospel to be eloquent because he wanted people's faith to rest in God's power, not in his human answers. God desires to give us understanding, and He encourages us to gain wisdom; but our answers will not have the biggest impact on the hearts of non-believers. However, our response to God could lodge itself so deeply into the human heart of others that they will not be able to shake it. And when the time comes when they find themselves in need of the Savior, they will remember the joy, excitement and passion that they saw Christ produce in our lives.

Just Jump In

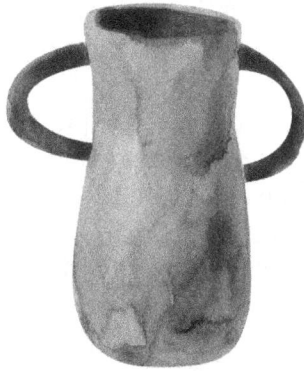

I love Peter. He is one of the coolest men in the New Testament, besides Jesus, of course! I'm a lot like Peter. I see Jesus walking on water, and I'm mesmerized. My eyes are fixed on Him, and I beg Him to call me into the waves. When Jesus finally calls me out of my safe boat, I jump into the water and take off running. About 10 seconds into my full-on sprint, I second guess myself and get distracted.

I see big waves all around me, I feel water spray hitting my face and I hear the wind angrily howling for me to stop. My pace starts to slow down, and I think, "What the heck are you doing, Alisa? You can't walk on water! You're going to drown!" And KERPLUNK! SPLASH! I fall into the water and go into "save my own skin" mode.

As I'm gulping water and gasping for air, Jesus comes to me calmly, picks me up, smiles and says, "You of little faith. Why did you doubt?"

I look up at Jesus and sheepishly say, "Well, at least I got out of the boat!"

Jesus sighs, smiles again and carries me (on water) back to the boat. He knows I'm not perfect, but I'm trying.

Are you sitting in the boat or are you begging for Jesus to tell you it's time to come out?

I don't think Jesus was disappointed because Peter jumped out of the boat and sank. I think Jesus knew how much Peter was capable of accomplishing, but Peter didn't trust himself or Jesus.

Jesus knows our potential because He put it there. We've just got to trust Him. Don't be scared to jump out of the boat for Jesus. He wouldn't tell you to jump if He knew you would sink. Not only does Jesus believe you can walk on water, He believes you can run up waves, backflip off whitecaps and do a victory dance all the way back to the boat. Why? Because that's God promise to you! God says that you can do all things through Christ who strengthens you (Philippians 4.13).

This promise is what distinguishes us from the rest of the world. Christians should be doing the most crazy, amazing things and the world should be gawking! We shouldn't be known for our self-righteousness or our judgmental attitudes. We should be known for our amazing feats, our love for others and our love for God.

Don't be scared! God has all the cosmos in His hand; I'm pretty sure He can handle your little (but important) life.

And whenever you fail, God will slip in His grace. God's grace fills in all the cracks of our imperfections. His grace mixed with our obedience is an extremely beautiful and powerful thing.

Be obedient today and jump out of your safe boat. Overcome your fear and prepare yourself for the ride of your life!

"For we live by faith, not by sight" (2 Corinthians 5.7 NIV).

The Lead Vocalist

I met her at the first writers' group that I held at my house about several years ago. She was an amazing woman of God surrounded by grace and humility. She dedicated her heart to writing devotionals for my ministry and several months later, God called her to be the women's minister at my church. I was honored and blessed to be under her leadership.

Along with being a writer, women's minister and church staff member, she also sang onstage with our church band. I would watch her sing and become irritated. I couldn't hear my friend's voice! She would only sing back up, and I, not being musically inclined, couldn't distinguish her from the others. I told her my frustrations about not being able to hear her, but she was content to use her voice to support the lead vocalist.

One Sunday morning my friend wasn't singing, and I finally heard it: her voice was missing! Although I couldn't discern her voice, I could definitely tell when it was absent.

I saw her the following week and exclaimed, "I heard it!"

"What?" She asked.

"The lack of your voice!" I yelled excitedly.

She looked at me for a moment puzzled, but then she smiled with understanding. In a small way, I finally felt like I could appreciate her singing talent.

This past Sunday morning, God had a very special gift in store for me. After many years, I finally heard my friend's voice. She sang lead vocals, and I bawled. All my makeup was off my face before the pastor even said one word. I listened to my friend sing, and I thanked God for the amazing ways He shows Himself to me. What a beautiful sight I beheld. She was singing for her mighty God! Her voice is forever imprinted on my heart.

As I reflect on that morning, I know that many people have trouble hearing God's voice. They recognize when it's missing, but they have never heard Him speak so powerfully that there was no doubt the words were from God. I once struggled with hearing God's voice, and I worried whether or not I was listening to the wrong one.

But something changed. I now hear God's voice loud and clear. He speaks to me through the Bible, the Holy Spirit and other Christians. He engulfs me with His presence, and He whispers to my spirit. What's different? Why has it become so easy to distinguish His voice? The answer is simple. When I put God center stage, He became the Lead Vocalist singing into my life. All that I am stays focused on God, and I've learned to discern His voice.

"God's voice thunders in marvelous ways; he does great things beyond our understanding" (Job 37.5 NIV).

Accustomed to Paradise

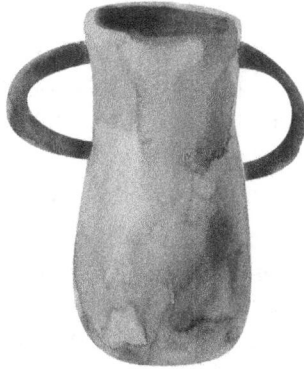

Brian "Head" Welch came to our church and talked about how he met Christ. I loved his testimony, which you can hear at I am Second. He "test drove the world," and he had everything that the world could offer: fame, money, women, success, etc. But a "dark cloud" hovered over his life, and he lived in misery. He thought he was a "loser," he was addicted to drugs and he couldn't care for his little girl.

But Jesus changed all that.

After Brian told us his redemption story, he expressed the amazing gift that we have in God. He said that Christianity is the only religion that offers a "Piece of Paradise" here on earth. The promised gift of the Holy Spirit comes to dwell in us once we receive forgiveness from Jesus Christ. Jesus took on our imperfection, so we could wear His perfection, and now we stand righteous before a perfect God. Because of grace, we are sanctified, and the Holy Spirit can live in us. This beautiful mystery of faith is the ultimate truth of Christianity.

Brian couldn't describe with words the peace and joy that flooded his life when he walked away from everything and followed after God. The world can give us its version of glory, but Brian explained that we were created to desire God. Nothing we consume will quench our yearning for God and His glory.

153

What moved me most about Brian's Holy Spirit-filled words was his delight and awe of God. Brian had found "paradise," and it was better than anything he had ever known. His excitement reminded me that I dwell in this paradise daily. I rest in green meadows and walk by peaceful streams (Psalm 23). God's presence is so much a part of my life that I think I sometimes forget what I have.

The Holy Spirit has been prompting me over and over again to remember what God has done in my life. I finally sat down and started from the time I was young, listing the amazing movement of His will in my mess. I thought about the times He protected and cared for me and when He guided and encouraged me. I looked at all the blessings in my life and saw how He has grown me and changed me into His image.

My transformation from an insecure 14-year old who was hopeless and lost to the strong Christian woman I am today is nothing short of miraculous. Changing from a person who hated reading and studying to becoming the learner and researcher I am now is shocking. God makes the fool wise and that is so obvious in my life. I am a fool who is wise only because God loves me, Christ died for me and the Holy Spirit guides me.

I don't want to take the "paradise" I have today for granted. I remember how I felt without Jesus, and I was miserable, purposeless and confused. Now I'm surrounded by peace, joy, love and hope that cannot be produced without God. I have paradise (a piece of God) inside of me, and that is a treasure worth selling everything for (Matthew 13.44).

"Remember the things I have done in the past. For I alone am God! I am God, and there is none like me" (Isaiah 46.9 NLT).

A Church Divided

I'm reading *Warriors Don't Cry*, a beautiful memoir written by Melba Pattillo Beals, one of the nine black students integrated into Little Rock's Central High in 1957. As I read about her childhood, I walked through memories that were vastly different from mine. She grew up in a "sepia-toned world, a cocoon of familiar people and places." The few times she interacted with white people tended to be racially charged and negative. As a child, she felt like a second-class citizen, but she and her family firmly believed that God would bring forth His justice and liberty.

I, on the other hand, grew up on a military base in the 1980s. I was surrounded by people of all skin tones and blends of hues. I had best friends who were white, black, Hispanic, Chinese and Filipino. I didn't believe we were all the same. I could see the differences in each culture first-hand, but I enjoyed and soaked up those differences. I never had to fight for my rights against an entire nation because I enjoyed the freedoms fought by those before me. Though our nation is far from perfect, we have experienced great victories won by people faithful to God's will.

I write all this because I'm learning that each of us has a unique lens on life. We can never assume that we know what someone is thinking or feeling, especially if we have limited our focus to ourselves. Though

Ms. Beals and I have unique upbringings and life-experiences, we both love and serve the same God. Our situation shapes our perspective on life, people and spirituality. Yet, God is able to form His love, mercy and grace to fit our personal needs and understanding.

I read a lot of books written by diverse spiritual leaders. Each leader has his/her unique Holy Spirit inspired passion and perspective. After reading a handful of books, I started to become nervous and confused. Every leader was so different and had diverse takes on the world, God and spirituality. I felt like there were huge spaces between each leader's spiritual ideology, and it was difficult for me to jump from one school of thought to another. But I knew every single one of them was aligned with God's Word and His Spirit. They each deepened my relationship with and understanding of God with strict Bible teachings.

Instead of pointing my "false prophet" finger, I kept reading more books. The Holy Spirit began bringing a colorful array of spiritual mentors into my path, and I consumed their insights. As I continued reading, other spiritual ideologies arose, and those big spaces between schools of thought became smaller and smaller. Soon these amazing, God-breathed insights formed stepping-stones that merged together to create a solid path to God. I discovered that every spiritual revelation tied together at the root of God and made up His beloved bride: the Church! And God wants us to live in harmony, so He can raise up His Bride that we may glorify Him.

"May the God of endurance and encouragement grant you to live in such harmony with one another, in accord with Christ Jesus, that together you may with one voice glorify the God and Father of our Lord Jesus Christ" (Romans 15.5-6 ESV).

My Mauve God

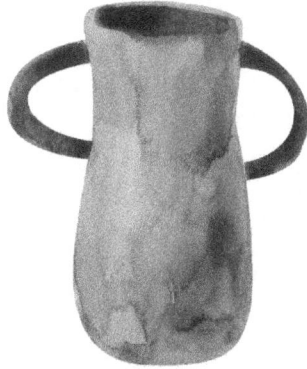

In 2010, I read a ton of books written by Christian leaders. I felt like God opened my mind, and the insights from these amazing men and women poured into my soul. However, something began to irritate me—I became a little jealous of God's glory in these people's lives. His Spirit shined in brilliant colors that seemed to overshadow my seemingly lackluster life.

For example, one leader saw the physical manifestation of Jesus during a very difficult time in his life. Another leader witnessed the outpouring of the Holy Spirit, which came down on his audience like fire. And another leader performed a miraculous healing with the power of Jesus' name. I began to feel inadequate because I had never experienced any of these things, and I desired so much to see God's glory in my life.

I contemplated all of this while I was helping my kids color at the kitchen table. I had just bought a jumbo box of crayons, and I was intrigued by all the shades of the same color. I felt the Holy Spirit tell me to pick a color. I chose pink. Then He told me to gather all the shades of pink I could find. He had me write the name of each crayon in its color on a piece of paper. By the time I was done writing all the shades of pink, I had a list of over 20 colors. I folded the paper and stuck it into the pocket of my jeans. I knew God was going to teach me something.

Once I put my kids to sleep for naptime, I went into my closet to pray and read my Bible. I felt the Holy Spirit tell me to take the list out and look at it. I unfolded it and looked from one color to the next, analyzing how each color name fit its shade. Some pinks were bright with a hint of orange. Others were bold with a lot of red. While others were so pale that they were almost transparent.

God asked me, "Which color do you like best?"

I scanned the list and chose mauve.

"Why do you like mauve," He asked.

"It's subtle, earthy and not overly showy," I said. Though I appreciated the brighter and richer shades of pink, I liked the easy-going, down-to-earth shade of mauve. It had a lot of purple in it, which is my favorite color.

"Mauve is my shade of love for you. It is how My glory appears in your life," God said. "I show Myself in the daily activities of your day—nothing out of the ordinary, but always very special."

I thought about it for a moment, and I understood what God was saying. I see God in everything around me: I see Him in a bird flying, I see Him in my kids, I see Him in a song on the radio, I see Him in my memories and my daily activities. I see Him in the small nuances of my life, and His glory in me is just as powerful and amazing as His glory in the prophet, the preacher and the healer. I see God face to face, and His presence lives in and through me. He is my Mauve God.

"The one sitting on the throne was as brilliant as gemstones—like jasper and carnelian. And the glow of an emerald circled his throne like a rainbow" (Revelation 4.3 NLT).

Beautiful Lack

I finally purged my closet.

It felt so good. I can't believe the piles of clothes, shoes and accessories that came out of that small space. At the end of my four-hour purge, I had three piles of trash and four piles of giveaway stuff. I looked at the mess in my room, and I knew all that unnecessary stuff had made getting dressed difficult and confusing every morning.

I got rid of old college t-shirts, clothes I bought on sale but never wore, shoes that were trendy but hurt my feet, belts and scarves that haven't been touched in years, and work clothes that I no longer needed. Every time I held an item in my hand and thought, "Well, maybe someday I'll wear it," I would throw it in a pile. If I'm not wearing it now, I will never wear it!

Once I cleaned out my closet, I discovered several nice pieces that I had forgotten about. They were pressed between clothes I usually ignored, so I never saw them. Also, there was now a ton of space in my closet, and it felt good to know that I was gaining control over my wardrobe. Style has never been my forte, but I'm beginning to learn that a few "perfect" items are better than a truckload of "okay" items.

With all that empty space, I began to get excited. Yes, I had very few clothes now, but I didn't see it as a lack—I saw it as an opportunity! I was determined to slowly fill the emptiness with clothes that fit my body type, lifestyle and personal taste. No longer would I cram stuff into my closet that obviously didn't belong there.

As I stared at my completed work, God said, "Isn't lack beautiful?"

I instantly knew what God was referring to. He had purged my life of everything that was "okay." I can remember every instance when He told me to throw something out or give something over to someone else. I felt insecure because I feared people's opinions of me. Would they think I was being lazy? Would they think I wasn't doing enough for God? Would they somehow think I was living in rebellion?

First of all, I know that I shouldn't put other people's opinions over God's because that is idolatry. Second of all, I finally discovered what God was doing when He cleaned out my life. He was getting rid of everything unnecessary because He was about to fill my life with perfectly tailored pieces of my destiny. I was in a beautiful lack, and I became excited about what God was about to do.

Have you ever been in a beautiful lack? Does God want to purge your life of all the distractions that pull you away from your purpose? Will you allow God to trash all the "okay" things that confuse your calling? Don't worry about what other people think about the purge—they'll understand when they see you walking in an amazing wardrobe tailored to your life. Hopefully, they'll learn from your example and do a little life-cleaning themselves.

"I know what it is to be in need, and I know what it is to have plenty. I have learned the secret of being content in any and every situation, whether well fed or hungry, whether living in plenty or in want" (Philippians 4.12 NIV).

160

Locusts and Honey

I used to have trouble hearing from the Holy Spirit; and from talking with other Christians, this is a common concern. Although the Holy Spirit doesn't answer all my questions and I don't understand many of my steps of obedience, I am now able to discern His voice more clearly.

I'm impressed by many figures in the Bible who received revelation from God. They didn't question whether or not they heard from Him; they stood firmly on His direction in their life. Job, Abraham, Gideon, Joseph, Moses, David and Paul all heard clearly from God and tried to follow His leading.

I know that sin can clog our ears from hearing the Holy Spirit, but I think there is another phenomenon plaguing Christians today, preventing us from hearing God's voice. We are bombarded with the Tree of Knowledge of Good and Evil. We have so much information streaming into our minds that we can't hear above the noise.

I believe that we could consume more information in one day than people from history's past could consume in one year.

While David spent his days watching sheep and cultivating his relationship with God as a youth, our children spend their days devouring video games, magazines, Internet sites, television shows, books, movies, music, texts and the influences of dozens of people in a single day. I don't believe any one of these things is wrong, but too much exposure to information is causing our brains to become overweight and our spirits to starve.

I started hearing from God when I turned off the TV, threw away the magazines, walked away from the computer, monitored my music, became picky about movies, guarded my choice of books and protected myself from the influences of others. I stopped the flow of the information dump into my life, and finally the voice of God sounded from the mountaintops!

I thought, "There You are, God!"

God told me, "I was always here!"

Now before I decide to consume information, I tell myself this statement: "Eat the locusts and God will give you honey."

Entomophagy means to eat insects as food, which includes both locusts and honey. John the Baptist ate locusts and honey when he lived in the wilderness and preached God's Word. Locusts are continually found in the Bible, usually seen as pests devouring crops (Exodus 10.14). Obviously, there were a lot of locusts, and John didn't need money to buy them. Even though John was the only son of a Levite mother and father and had the ability to consume the choicest meats given as sacrifice, he settled for the bug.

However, John also ate honey. Honey is also found in the Bible and is used in reference to the abundance of the Promised Land (Deuteronomy 26.15), to cheer people up (1 Samuel 14.29), in celebration (Song of Solomon 5.1) and to describe God's Word (Ezekiel 3.3 and Psalm 19.10). I find it interesting that John topped off his day of bug munching with an amazing batch of wild honey!

I thought, "If honey represents God's Word, I want some more!"

God said, "Then start eating locusts, and you'll have more room for my honey!"

What I've discovered is that whenever I choose to avoid the delicacies of the world, God blesses me with His honey. Every time I sacrifice my cravings for what the world serves up, God is able to feed me with His glory. I'm learning to cater my appetite to spiritual things because I know that my life on this earth is short, and I don't want to be on my deathbed with a stomach full of the world. I want more of God in my life.

I choose to eat locusts, so God can bless me with more honey.

"Their destiny is destruction, their god is their stomach, and their glory is in their shame. Their mind is on earthly things" (Philippians 3.19 NIV).

Stretching

As I build my physical strength, I've noticed that I hurt more. I'll do something seemingly easy, and I'll sprain, twist or pull something. My back begins to hurt, and I wonder why building muscle is not preventing these aches and pains.

I finally figured out that I'm not flexible. The strength training I'm doing is great, but it needs to be accompanied with stretching all the tendons and ligaments that connect my muscles and bones. If one area of my body becomes stronger, the weakness in other areas becomes painfully obvious—literally.

I've begun to stretch. I stretch while watching the kids play, before or after my time with God, even during a family movie night. Finally, I've noticed a difference in my performance. I don't hurt as much, and my aches and pains have lessened because my body is better able to withstand the stress.

I have noticed this same connection in my spiritual life. Many times, Christians work hard at building our strength spiritually, yet we get hurt easily. Someone says something or does something, and we immediately take offense. Something happens in our lives and we get offended at God. We become strong Christians who are weak with mercy, grace and loyalty.

Christians can be spiritual powerhouses all they want; but if they're groveling over all the offenses they receive, they'll never fulfill their destiny to the fullest. We gain our greatest range of motion when we are flexible.

I don't know about you, but I'm tired of being offended. I want to shine glory on God's throne, so I'm determined to allow God to stretch me until it is uncomfortable—even a bit painful. But I know that when He is done, I won't find myself hurting all of the time. I trust God's hand in my life, and I will lean on Him instead of clinging onto hurt.

"Whoever would foster love covers over an offense, but whoever repeats the matter separates close friends (Proverbs 17.9 NIV).

Crown or Ashes

In 2 Samuel 13, the lovely princess, Tamar, was raped by her half-brother. To show her disgrace she put ashes on her head (2 Samuel 13.19). Ashes represent self-disgust, humility or grief and they are a physical representation of the pain or guilt one feels.

I've had to wear ashes many times, but the problem came when I never washed them off. I would make a mistake, get hurt or feel sorrow, and I would smear that pain all over my body. The ashes affected every aspect of my life, and I couldn't be the princess God wanted to shine His glory through because I was covered in soot.

I used to feel like that was the way it was supposed to be until God confronted me. He asked, "Is the blood on the cross not strong enough to wash you clean?" Hebrews 9.14 reads, "How much more, then, will the blood of Christ, who through the eternal Spirit offered himself unblemished to God, cleanse our consciences from acts that lead to death, so that we may serve the living God!" (NIV). I realized that whenever I clung unto my grief, I was telling God that He wasn't strong enough to redeem me. Also, I became useless in serving Him.

In Isaiah 61.3 (NIV), God says that He will "bestow on them a crown of beauty instead of ashes." I don't think that we can quite fathom this exchange. We hand over our ashes and God gives us a beautiful crown instead? How could that be? It is only possible because God has an unquenchable and unshakable love for us. We live in a broken world where people get hurt, and God knows this. So He beautifully matches our shame with His grace to compensate for the sin surrounding us. However, we have free will to receive God's grace or reject it.

God never promised this life would be easy, but He does offer us His grace in a broken world and blesses us when we love and obey Him (Deuteronomy 30.11-19). I don't know about you, but I'm tired of wearing my shame. I want to surround myself by beautiful crowns; so when I see Jesus at His throne, I can throw them at His feet. Let us start gathering God's grace instead of our shame, so we can do the mighty work that God has planned for us.

"Stalwart walks in step with God; his path blazed by God, he's happy. If he stumbles, he's not down for long; God has a grip on his hand" (Psalm 37.23 MSG).

Obedience Blur

About a year ago, God asked me to stop going to the gym. This was upsetting for me because I have gone to the gym ever since I was a young adult. I love working out, and the gym atmosphere motivates me and ensures that I exercise. I couldn't understand why God would ask me to take this step of obedience.

Because I no longer had a gym membership, I had to squeeze in my workouts at home. My four to five times a week exercise routine shortened to two or three days. It became increasingly difficult to find time to exercise with three kids at home. I would beg my husband to watch the kids while I jogged. I would work out on an exercise step outside while the kids played. I would work out while the kids napped or after they went down for the night.

My workouts began to eat away my writing time, and I struggled with not being able to effectively do both. I couldn't figure out how to balance my schedule, and I started to feel like I wasn't able to handle all of my responsibilities.

Finally, I became fed up. I decided I was going to wake up an hour earlier each morning. I already woke up about 30 minutes before my kids so I could do a quiet time, but now I was determined to work out and spend time with God before my kids came looking for me.

The first day, I dragged myself downstairs and did a workout video. Afterward, I felt so great, and I had an excellent time with God because I was wide awake and filled with energy! By the time my kids were up, I was ready for the day. I didn't have any bad mommy moments that day because I no longer had an agenda to keep. I wrote while the kids slept, but other than that, I was completely there for them.

What I learned from this experience is that many times our steps of obedience take us into a period of confusion or imbalance. This is normal because we are adjusting to our new situation that the change has created. I think many times we turn away from our obedience because we falsely believe that the transition should have been easy. The fact is that many things we do for God are not easy, but God always has a wonderful purpose.

It took me an entire year to finally adjust to my small step of obedience. And although life still does not play out perfectly each day, I have found the balance that I knew God wanted me to achieve. I'm sure He cheered for me the entire time, and I'm glad that I trusted His will for my life.

"Be thankful in all circumstances, for this is God's will for you who belong to Christ Jesus" (1 Thessalonians 5.18 NLT).

Soccer Humility

My sister-in-law has been inviting me to play city-league soccer with her for several years. This season I finally felt ready, so I went out and bought my cleats, shin guards, and soccer ball. I am thirty-two years old, and I have never played a lick of soccer (save elementary gym class) in my entire life.

When I met the other team members, it became painfully obvious that I was soccer ignorant. I needed help putting on my shin guards, my sister-in-law had to give me a quick lesson on how to kick the ball (on the side of your shoelaces), I had to be told over and over again the name of each position, and my teammates had to continually tell me where to stand on the field.

My ignorance became evident to the other team, as well. During the game, the ball went over the goal, and I asked a player that I was guarding if it was good or not. She looked at me with surprise and said, "It has to go into the goal to be good." As the girl laughed and walked off, I struggled with my utter stupidity. I finally decided to swallow my pride (it kept catching in my throat), and I worked harder to do better.

I turned my focus to the ball. I might not have all the fancy footwork that every woman around me seemed born with, but I had the determination and a learning spirit. I blocked the ball, kicked it (maybe not quite in the direction of my teammate), hit the ball with my head (well, it was actually the side of my face), and pestered any woman on the opposite team that had the ball. Even though I was clueless, I became a crazy force to be reckoned with.

I played the entire game. I could feel my heart thumping against my chest, and I could have taken my pulse just by feeling the pulsating in my gums. My entire body was throbbing. I never realized how enormous the soccer field was and how few players there were on the field. The other team was so good at passing the ball that it felt like I was always chasing it. The other team won, but I knew that I didn't make it easy for them.

I motivated myself by saying, "Glory to God! Glory to God!"

I knew that many of the women were not Christians, so I wanted to be a good example of persistence and dedication. I wasn't going to let the fact that I knew nothing of soccer stop me from playing it. I know that God loves me and thinks I'm special, so if the entire world of soccer laughs at me, I would be okay. My desire is to base my self-worth on being a daughter of God, not on what the world thinks of me. And if I do that, I can do anything.

If we as God's daughters and sons base our entire self-worth on the awesome fact that we are His, we can do anything! So many Christians fear doing something new. We don't want to join a Bible study, volunteer at our church, go to a new playdate or share our faith with others because we are scared of what people will think of us. But we can't let fear stop us from stepping out because God is always doing something new: "See, I am doing a new thing! Now it springs up; do you not perceive it? I am making a way in the desert and streams in the wasteland" (Isaiah 43.19 NIV).

In our Christian walk, God will always have us reach outside of our comfort zone. Whenever we start to feel comfortable, we must prepare ourselves—God is going to do something new. The best way for us to perceive what He is doing and to be ready for it is by swallowing our

171

pride and humbling ourselves. We can't always be know-it-alls. We can't always be the best. We can't always have it all together.

Often times, we will be ignorant and on the bottom of the barrel. But that's okay! Our self-worth is based on the fact that we are children of God: "Now if we are children, then we are heirs—heirs of God and co-heirs with Christ, if indeed we share in his sufferings in order that we may also share in his glory" (Romans 8.17 NIV). This promise should be enough to encourage our complete obedience and dependence on God.

Jesus came to this earth as a lowly carpenter. He served people every day by healing the sick, feeding the hungry and teaching the uninformed. He washed His disciples' feet and sacrificed His body for the world. He could have come to this earth as a Prince, demanding angels and humans to do His bidding and expecting us to pay for our own sins. But He didn't! He humbled Himself for us and did something new, and we are called to follow His example!

"Humility and the fear of the LORD bring wealth and honor and life" (Proverbs 22.4 NIV).

Glory Color

I've been thinking a lot about how God designed me—well, actually, I've been complaining. I trust that God has designed me in a specific way, so I can fulfill a specific purpose in life. I love to write, and I know that writing is a big part of my design and plan. However, as I look over each of my posts and read what I have written, I can't help but think, "Dang it, Alisa! You are always so serious!"

I remember one time I got so sick of my melancholy writing that I wrote a brilliantly funny post (at least in my mind). I always enjoyed women who wrote funny blog posts, and I so appreciate their gift-offering of a smile and a laugh. So on my funny post I wrote about my boys peeing off the deck. I couldn't wait to read the comments.

That night when I tried to sleep, I felt Holy Spirit tell me to take the post off my blog. I tried ignoring the Holy Spirit and later rationalized His words. Finally, though, I flung the covers off me, stumbled to the computer room and deleted my wonderfully witty post. And God sat me down and told me, "You write for me alone."

"Yes, God," I whispered and crawled back into bed.

Later, as I was thinking over these things, my identical twin sister called me with a spiritual breakthrough God had given her. My sister

173

and I look a lot alike, but the core of who we are, how we view life and how we interact with God are completely different. Our perspectives are so unique that we have to discuss everything to pieces just to ensure that there are no misunderstandings that would translate into hurt feelings.

She admitted that reading my blog and reading other Christian writers' blogs made her feel that she was spiritually lagging—that maybe her relationship with Christ wasn't as strong. But what she realized is that her purpose is very different than mine and the writers she has been reading, so her interactions with God and her understanding of spirituality will also be different. She decided that there is nothing wrong with not always being so serious, and I wanted to yell out, "Thank God! I can barely handle my own seriousness!"

My sister is positive and funny. She makes people laugh and feel comfortable. She goes out of her way to ensure harmony, and she does it all to the glory of God!

I truly think that when God created people, He fitted each of us with a tiny and unique slice of His glory. I imagine God's glory as a giant ball of a million-billion colors—colors that we can't even comprehend on this earth. And He placed an individual hue of His multi-colored beauty into each of His children. Yes, some of the hues may look very similar from a distance; but on closer inspection, they are each very distinct.

Our mission is to shine our tiny color of God's glory to the world and fight the urge to blend in with the other colors around us. My twin sister's glory-color may be a golden-pink and my glory-color may be a silvery-blue, and our lens of life will be tinted by our colors. That is why it is so important for us not to judge and compare. God gave us each a unique design and purpose. We will all express love differently, reveal God's glory differently, relate to spiritual truths differently and interact with Jesus differently. But if we are seeking to know God more, there is no wrong answer—just wonderful variety.

I can imagine God in His million-billion color grandeur gathering up

His children in His arms; and once we are resting against the pulse of His heart, we each simultaneously shoot out our own glory-color, creating a miniature replica of His majesty. We are each created in the image of God, and we daily become more Christ-like and beautiful by letting go of sin. Maybe we should stop trying to change people and stop trying to change ourselves and start allowing God's glory to shine through the design He intended us to be.

"I'm praying not only for them but also for those who will believe in me because of them and their witness about me. The goal is for all of them to become one heart and mind—just as you, Father, are in me and I in you, so they might be one heart and mind with us. Then the world might believe that you, in fact, sent me. The same glory you gave me, I gave them, so they'll be as unified and together as we are—I in them and you in me. Then they'll be mature in this oneness, and give the godless world evidence That you've sent me and loved them in the same way you've loved me" (John 17.20-23 MSG).

A Stump

As you read through the final chapters of Exodus, you will find God's very particular blueprint for His worship place. From the material, design, usage, accents and construction—each aspect of the His holy dwelling was unique and intricate. After reading such detailed instructions, you might say, "Geez, God! You have pretty picky expectations!"

We are the New Testament Temple, and I want to say that God is just as picky about you (His chosen one) today as He was about His chosen people back then. You are His worship place; He dwells in you, and He has a plan for the temple He has given you.

If you daily seek God, you will find that He will give you detailed instructions. Some instructions are lasting, some are seasonal and some are for the moment; but He has a design, a purpose and a bunch of awe-inspiring accents that He wants to carve into your life. But you have to be obedient and let Him wield the hammer.

In my life, God has given me finite laws that go beyond the 10 Commandments. The 10 commandments are the basic moral foundation for all humanity; however, God's children have very explicit commandments. These laws shape our temples and make us unique and fruitful creations fashioned by God: "A life devoted to things is a dead life, a stump; a God-shaped life is a flourishing tree" (Proverbs 11.28 MSG).

I've come to realize that a God-shaped life can be a disciplined life. I have a list of things that I can't do. I sacrifice those things for God because I know that He has amazing blessings for me that far outweigh what I have given up for Him. I also have a list of things that I must do, but I have found joy that is not based on my circumstances. I now enjoy doing tasks that I once deemed as boring, difficult or trivial. I trust God, and I want Him to mold me; otherwise, I'll be molded by the world or the insignificance of my own understanding.

So my encouragement to you when God tells you to give up something or to do something, there is a purpose. God has a plan, and He has to make a particular pattern in your life because He is creating your temple to hold the beauty and power of His glory. Your pattern will be different from other people; but don't worry, they're getting shaped in other ways.

Do you want your life to be filled with God's glory? Do you want to be more than a stubby "stump" stuck in the trappings of this world? Then forget about what everyone else is doing and live within the parameters that God has tailored for your life. Stay focused on how the Holy Spirit is leading you this day and stay obedient to where He is directing the fullness of your life. Walk in discipline; and at the end of your days on earth, your life will be a gorgeous, fruit-filled tree.

"No discipline seems pleasant at the time, but painful. Later on, however, it produces a harvest of righteousness and peace for those who have been trained by it" (Hebrews 12.11 NIV).

Confusing One-Liners

I enjoy jogging on a certain main street in my neighborhood. A lot of joggers, skateboarders, and cyclists make their way down this road. The etiquette while jogging is to nod and say hello as you pass another jogger. If one is feeling very festive, she can try to squeeze in a fast one-liner during the few seconds of contact.

For example, one could say, "Windy day. Can't wait to go back the other way" or "I forgot that summer has arrived already" or "Wonder if I can call a cab to pick me up." These are quick little remarks that entertain the joggers as they sweat out all their frustration and that morning's donut. The comments are not terribly witty or remarkable; rather, they mainly work as creative little fillers.

I always wear my headphones and jam out to Christian music while I jog. Whenever I see another jogger in the distance, I turn off the music so I can respond to whatever is being said or I can make a remark if so inclined.

However, one particular afternoon I didn't want to turn off my radio. I was in a runner's groove, and I didn't feel like slowing down to look at my IPod. I decided that I would just speak to the passerby with the music playing in my ears. I prepared a quick comment about the weather and rehearsed it in my head. I was confident that I could give my small one-liner, make eye contact with the jogger and continue running my course. Simple.

Since the music was so loud in my ears, I really couldn't hear how I sounded, but it was obvious the other jogger had no idea what I had said. All I saw as I ran past him was an expression of confusion and a little shock on his face. I'm horrified to think about what noises came out of my mouth.

Many times, we as Christians do the same thing. We want to tell someone about Jesus, but we are listening to the loud noises of the world and we are unable to articulate clearly. We want to explain our relationship with Christ, but our words come out all jumbled and confused. Sometimes our entire life is one chaotic mess because we can't distinguish God's voice from among the world's racket.

I've realized that in my own walk with God, I have to tune out a lot of the world. Much of what I filter is not necessarily deemed as evil—it's just distracting. Once I started turning down the ruckus filling my ears, I was much better at hearing from the Lord. When I could hear God's voice, I became better at sharing His insights with others.

I know that God's grace covers all my mess-ups, but I would like to do a better job at focusing my radar on Him. I want to clearly hear God's voice, so He can do a mighty work in my life. If I could be diligent enough to tune-out the world's transmissions, my ears will have greater ability to receive God's holy signal, which is filled to overflowing with truth and promises.

"My Sheep hear my voice, and I know them, and they follow me" (John 10.27 ESV).

Foot Promises

Instead of dividing time by years, I try to envision all existence as one beautiful gift. Life is a single, intricate creation, bound together by a Name that we tend to whisper about–Jesus, Messiah, Christ, Lord. Jesus was at God's side during our world's *inception*, He hung on the cross at its *redemption* and, finally, He'll break through the skies at its *completion*.

Jesus stands firmly in the center of creation, watching as His divine purpose comes to fruition. He takes small but amazing pieces of His will and places them at His feet. They are called His promises. Then He puts the desire for those promises in each of us.

The promises are beyond our abilities, but we are drawn to them like a magnet to metal. The world tries to sidetrack us with tantalizing distractions that urge us to wander. As we seek Jesus, though, He compels us forward by faith.

We struggle onward in a life that isn't easy. We learn to rely on the joy, peace and hope found in the core of God's spirit in us as Christians. We slowly loosen our grip on the world, and we walk into the unknown, holding onto the only truth that we can rely on: We are loved. Though our bodies, minds and hearts grow weary, our souls attain supernatural rest in Him.

When we finally arrive at our promises, we realize that they were only the lures. We walked by faith to the feet of Jesus, and He skimmed off our sin in the process. We now understand the purpose of our pain and the significance of our struggle. We look up at the face of Jesus and hand Him the weight of our promises, and He pulls us up into the power, the majesty and the beauty of His glory.

"'For I know the plans I have for you,' says the Lord. 'They are plans for good and not for disaster, to give you a future and a hope'" (Jeremiah 29.11 NLT).

Do Nothing

Today, I began reading the story of Jesus sleeping through the storm. The storm was bad enough to scare seasoned fishermen. These men have probably seen pretty intense storms, yet this one could have killed them. Though the situation was dire, Jesus did nothing to save their lives. The disciples had to wake Jesus and beg Him to intervene, and Jesus was none too happy about it: "He said to his disciples, 'Why are you so afraid? Do you still have no faith?'" (Mark 4.40 NIV).

I also read about the first Easter and realized the two stories are very similar. Jesus allowed the world to kill Him, yet He did nothing to stop them. There was a spiritual storm going on, but Jesus would not intervene. Jesus knew that His Crucifixion was a part of God's purpose. He had to have faith and relent to God's will.

After I read both stories, I felt the Holy Spirit tell me, "Sometimes I *want you to do nothing.*"

I've experienced storms in my life in which I fought, begged and struggled. I realize in retrospect that I should have done nothing. I fought against situations, I begged God to help me and I struggled with people; but I should have just taken a catnap and let God deal with it. I needed to *be still* and meditate on God's greatness (Psalm 46.10).

God has battles He has anointed us to fight, and He promises us that He will go before us and claim our victory (Deuteronomy 20.4). However, there are battles that He will fight for us. There are situations, people and storms that God will take care of on our behalf, and He doesn't want us to lift a finger (Psalm 35.1). But we need to trust Him.

Sitting on our hands and trusting God is sometimes more painful than battling against everyone who persecutes us. We need to follow Jesus' example: Sometimes He confronted and other times He relented. Jesus trusted God's divine will.

All we have to do is stay in tuned with the Holy Spirit's leading. Is He telling us to prepare for battle or to prepare for bed? If we can pick and choose our battles based on God's ultimate design, we will not become weary with defending ourselves all the time. God promises us that He will redeem us; we just need to have faith in His Word.

Jesus did so many amazing things, and He was busy much of the time. However, He knew when He needed to work and when He needed to rest. If we could find that balance, we would reserve energy for the times God calls us to action. God does us a favor when He tells us to rest during the conflicts. He knows we can do nothing because the victory is already His.

God allows certain storms to arise because they are a part of His master plan. If we fight against everything that attacks us, we might be accidentally resisting God: "But if it is from God, you will not be able to stop these men; you will only find yourselves fighting against God" (Acts 5.39 NIV). So let us rest in His presence while He does the fighting for us!

Swimming in Canals

I was jogging down one of my neighborhood's main streets, which bridges over a canal. I felt God telling me to stop at a point on the sidewalk that looked over the middle of the water. I looked down and watched the canal curve and stretch before me. It was going in a different direction than my current path, and it led into a part of the bay that I didn't quite know.

God said, "You're about to jump."

Of course, I knew God didn't mean for me to physically jump, but He was alluding to some kind of change in my life. A change that I was going to have to jump into. I was excited. I have several God-promises on the back burners just waiting to be served. I couldn't wait to find out what life circumstances God was going to shake up.

A day later, I read a book that has changed my life. As I read each chapter, it felt like a door was being opened in my mind—a door that I had closed and forgotten about. While reading, I had to take little naps because the Holy Spirit was doing a lot of rewiring in my mind and spirit, and I was exhausted.

I didn't understand what was going on, but I knew it was special. My entire outlook on who I was in Christ and my relationship with Him began to focus with clarity, but this focus shot me into the depths of the unknown. After finishing the book, I realized that I had jumped from the bridge into the canal. I found myself flailing about in the water not knowing what to do next. I thought God was going to change my circumstances. I didn't know He was just going to change me.

What do you do when you jump into a canal? You swim. I'm determined to swim in this new awareness that God has given me, and I know that it's part of my route to Jesus. I'm excited and intimidated about growing into this new stage of Christlikeness, but I'm ready for the challenge. I want to know God on a deeper level, and I'm willing to make the sacrifices to do so.

I'm realizing that this change is more important than any change in my circumstances. I know that God can and does use circumstances to change us, but I'm eager to try out a change that can't be seen with the human eye. I want a spiritual change; one that is initiated by the Holy Spirit and received by my obedience. I'm still learning, but I'm figuring out that Jesus is the core of all existence. He is the seed of life. If I can grow into my awareness of Him and into the fullness of who I am in Him, I believe that I'll be on the right path.

"For by him all things were created: things in heaven and on earth, visible and invisible, whether thrones or powers or rulers or authorities; all things were created by him and for him. He is before all things, and in him all things hold together. And he is the head of the body, the church; he is the beginning and the firstborn from among the dead, so that in everything he might have the supremacy. For God was pleased to have all his fullness dwell in him, and through him to reconcile to himself all things, whether things on earth or things in heaven, by making peace through his blood, shed on the cross" (Colossians 1.16-20 NIV).

Kingdom is Here

As I was studying the Scriptures tonight about what I feel the Holy Spirit is calling me to write, God humbled and enlightened me. I wanted to write about the criminal on the cross who hung next to Jesus. Out of everyone who was with Jesus during His ministry, this man was the only one who got it.

Jesus' disciples, the religious leaders and the current culture of the time were waiting for a new King David to free the Jewish people from their oppression. They were looking for a warrior king to establish their earthly kingdom. They didn't realize that Jesus was establishing an eternal kingdom (Matthew 25.34), which came straight from the paradise of God (Revelation 2.7). This Kingdom is far greater than the kingdom the people fervently desired. They just couldn't see it, but the criminal did.

The criminal reached out to Jesus in the shortest salvation prayer that I've ever heard:

"Then he said, 'Jesus, remember me when you come into your kingdom'" (Luke 23.42 NIV).

Jesus is so amazing because this man took one tiny step of faith toward Him, and Jesus made up the difference. Jesus confirmed this man's timid request with a mighty promise:

"Jesus answered him, 'I tell you the truth, today you will be with me in paradise'" (Luke 23.43 NIV).

I was going to write tonight that the reason this criminal hanging on his cross next to Jesus was able to get it—why He was able to understand that the new Kingdom was not of this earth—was because he was on his deathbed. Nothing gives us more clarity about eternity then when we are about to enter it. However, the Holy Spirit told me otherwise.

For us to believe that we will enter the Kingdom of Heaven only after we die is extremely egocentric. It would be like saying the Kingdom of Heaven's existence is dependent on us. But it is not. God gave Jesus the keys to the Kingdom of Heaven, and Jesus already opened it with His death and resurrection. I believe the criminal on the cross knew the Kingdom of Heaven was at hand not because he was about to die, but because Jesus was about to die.

The Kingdom of Heaven was established and is in existence now. We are walking in it, breathing in it and living in it. We received our place in this Kingdom when we prayed for Jesus to come into our hearts and forgive us of our sins. Since our sinful flesh prohibits us from entering this Kingdom physically, God placed the Kingdom into each Christian (Luke 17.21). Our spirits are redeemed by Jesus' sacrifice for our sins and are now resting on a hammock by the Shores of Paradise.

What does this mean for us? How do we conduct ourselves knowing that our spirit is already dwelling in the Kingdom of Heaven? The following verse gave me some clarity.

"I will give you the keys of the kingdom of heaven; and whatever you bind (declare to be improper and unlawful) on earth must be what is already bound in heaven; and whatever you loose (declare lawful) on earth must be what is already loosed in heaven" (Matthew 16.19 AMP).

Since Jesus' death on the cross already established the Kingdom of

Heaven and that Kingdom—which comes from the core of God—has already been placed in each of us, shouldn't we be living like it? I try to imagine that I'm always at the foot of the throne, even if I can't see it with my human eyes. There are no secrets from God. He sees everything. God desires to love us, and He's willing to pour out His grace on all of our mistakes so He can hold us near to Him. All we have to do is allow God to embrace us and not try to wiggle free from Him. When we draw close to God, we find ourselves in complete joy (Kingdom of Heaven), and we realize that the worldly happiness we begged God for was counterfeit (earthly kingdom).

My spirit at this very moment exists in God's established Kingdom. I'm sitting on a swivel chair, typing on a computer smack-dab in the middle of Paradise. I just need to get my flesh to wake up to that fact. I want to yoke myself to Jesus every moment, so He will anchor my spirit-awareness to His Kingdom. I don't want to wander off and realize that I've stumbled yet again into the kingdom of this earth, which is controlled by the enemy.

I choose life. I choose joy. I choose paradise.

Because Jesus already gave them to me, I claim them now.

Not King of Slaves

Jesus is the King of Kings, not the King of Slaves. We are children of God and co-heirs with Christ (Romans 8.17). We are called to be kings of an inheritance created and given to us before the world began. Yet, many Christians live as slaves. We are slaves to the world, instead of free by His truth (John 8.32).

We each have a passion to lead, but our preconceived and corrupted beliefs prevent us from knowing the truth about who we are in Christ. We fill our minds with the lies of the world and the promises of God stay locked up in our unread Bibles and godless thoughts.

The only way to discover our royal heritage is to leave the yoke of slavery and head towards the Promised Land (Ephesians 1.11). However, many Christians fear the wilderness that they must pass through in order to reach freedom. We stay content in our honey-like pleasures and trapped in our mediocre mindsets. We are kings living as slaves by choice.

Why must we pass through the wilderness in order to reach the Promised Land? The wilderness teaches us how to be kings. The wilderness helps us to shed our chains and embrace the passion and purpose that God has placed in each one of us. Most of all, however, the wilderness teaches us the true definition of kingship.

189

Jesus Christ is the King of Kings and the Lord of Lords, and He came to this earth to serve. The inheritance that God has for you—the kingdom that He has created for you—is your ultimate gift of service to this world. You were built to serve humankind in a specific area. The more you are able to serve, the bigger your kingdom will grow (Mark 9.35).

It is God-like to serve the needs of others. It is slave-like to be served. If you feel like you are not fulfilling your purpose in life, you may have not found your current niche in which you have the power to serve. If you feel like your kingdom is not growing, you may not be fully embracing the privilege of serving others.

God has a plan for your life. When you find your gift of service, God will give you grace and power to multiply your efforts beyond what you can humanly manufacture. Our life is short and there are distractions around every corner. God has placed in your spirit a desire for your life to have meaning and for you to live out a purpose. Seek His will. Discover your destiny. You will find passion that you didn't know was in you. You'll wake each day with a confidence that you can't explain and a fire that the world can't smother.

"They will make war against the Lamb, but the Lamb will overcome them because he is Lord of lords and King of kings—and with him will be his called, chosen and faithful followers" (Revelation 17.14 NIV).

Silence in the Storm

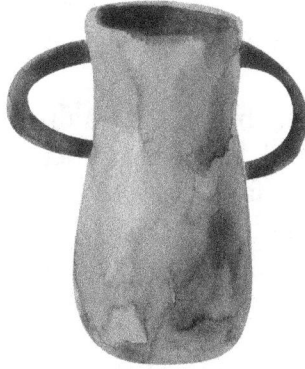

During Jesus' day, disciples (students) didn't just go to school and learn from their teachers. They immersed themselves into their teacher's life. They followed their teacher almost every moment of every day. This is true for Jesus' twelve disciples. They were always with Jesus.

They experienced all the miracles firsthand that Jesus performed. Each miracle I read, I believe in my heart that it is a historical fact that has been recorded into the Living Word of God. I don't doubt what the Bible says; however, that doesn't mean that I have faith in them. Belief and faith are two totally different claims.

As I was reading in my one-year Bible, I came across another of Jesus' miracles: "Then he stood up and told the wind to be silent, the sea to quiet down: 'Silence!' The sea became smooth as glass" (Matthew 8.26 MSG). Jesus and His disciples were floating in the middle of a severe storm. The disciples believed they were drowning, and Jesus was taking a nap on the deck.

After Jesus spoke peace into this middle of this storm, The Message Bible reads in verse 27, "The men [disciples] rubbed their eyes, astonished. 'What's going on here? Wind and sea come to heel at his command!'"

Just that day Jesus had healed a leper, the Centurion's servant who was not even present, the "inwardly tormented" and the "bodily ill." Why all of a sudden did the disciples rub their eyes? What had changed to cause them to ask, "What's going on here?" They had seen Jesus do miracles. They had belief, but they still lacked faith.

The distinction between belief and faith occurs when the miracle needed becomes personal. It is easy to believe victory over someone else's storm, but it takes faith to claim victory over your own storm. God is teaching me faith because I'm learning to claim victory in my own storms while the waves of life are crashing on me, causing me to want to give up and drown.

Faith is hard because everywhere I look, all I see is impossibility and hopelessness. I don't see an answer in the physical, but I need to claim God's solution in the spiritual. The storm is causing me to feel pain, worry, mistrust, fear and anger; but I need to take those thoughts captive and claim victory (2 Corinthians 10.5). The physical world is merely a manifestation of what's going on in the spiritual world. If I can shout victory in the spirit by faith, God can take that mustard seed of faith and create the solution (Matthew 17.20)!

What storm are you in the middle of today? A finance storm? A marriage storm? A job storm? A ministry storm? An inward storm? You are the eye of the storm. The storm wouldn't be there if you didn't exist. Don't just believe that God can do a miracle. Have faith that God is producing a miracle from the storm's center—you. Stand up in faith and allow the Holy Spirit within to claim "Silence" over the storm.

Rock or a Frog

I woke up early this morning to get some writing done before the day started. Lately, the days have been filled to the brim with activity, leaving me with only a few hours alone before dawn.

My dachshund, Rusty, realized I was up and came into my office. He sat down and stared at me for a brief moment before barking at me to take him outside. I quickly got up and hushed him to keep his burly voice down. I didn't want the kids to wake up and commence the day too early.

I walked him to the back door and opened it. He hurriedly jumped out, heading for the crisp, green grass. But before he made it off of the cement patio, he began to sniff. I heard a little "ribbit, ribbit." I looked over and saw a frog the size of a Hot Wheels truck, sitting on his haunches and croaking in the early morning.

The frog must have seen Rusty coming his way, because he instantly pushed his entire body down on the ground, closed his eyes and stopped croaking. As Rusty sniffed at him, the frog laid absolutely still. Not a peep could be heard or a single movement could be seen. Since my dog loves to chase things, I was sure he would go after this little frog. But after a few moments of sniffing and waiting, Rusty finally gave up and made his way to the lawn.

I was just about to head back into the house, but I glanced at the frog one last time. I thought maybe I was mistaken. Maybe I hadn't seen a frog after all. I walked over to the frog and stared as he stayed unmoving on the patio. From a closer view, I could definitely tell that he was a frog, but he almost looked like a rock sitting there.

What a smart frog! Because the frog did not move or croak, Rusty had gotten bored with him and wandered off to do his business. And I realized that this is exactly what we need to do as Christians when we feel like we are being spiritually attacked—stay very still and quiet!

We have an enemy who enjoys making a ruckus in our lives. He would like nothing better than to chase us around and cause us to panic. However, if we simply stay firm on God's Word and His promises, we won't have to run around like crazy people. We can simply close our eyes, lower our voices and wait patiently on the Lord.

"Wait patiently for the LORD. Be brave and courageous. Yes, wait patiently for the LORD" (Psalm 27:14 NLT).

Construction of a Dream

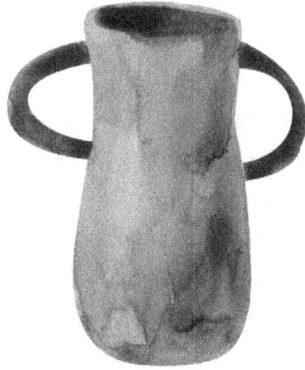

There is a house near my neighborhood that has been in the process of construction for over three years. This Christmas will mark its third season of empty holidays—no family to fill it, no fireplace to warm it, no Christmas decoration to trim it— completely and utterly alone. But this state of emptiness does not mean that it has been idle. On the contrary, busy hands have been methodically building this home for endless days. The foundation alone took a full year, and the structure of the house took another year!

Every time I pass this house, I'm amazed at what has been accomplished but keenly aware that it is not ready yet. To say this home is a mammoth is an understatement. And to say that it has been hurriedly constructed would be the opposite of the truth. In fact, the design of the house has obviously been well planned and every detail of construction has been scrutinized. The foundation goes deep and the structure of the home is made of steel, not wood. This house is being made to last centuries, not just a single lifetime!

But...

I wonder if the family has grown impatient to move in.

I wonder if they have lost hope of ever stepping foot into their dream home.

I wonder if they have visited the construction site to encourage themselves.

As I look at this home, I find understanding for my own impatience, and I'm able to tighten my faith around a deeper hope. Many times, God gives us promises that seem like they will never be fulfilled. We work diligently in obedience to the Holy Spirit and we remain patient to His timing, but after years and years and endless days, we wonder if we will ever step foot into our Promised Land. We have trouble seeing the finished product, and our hope begins to falter. We want to give up, but the time, energy and resources we have poured into our dream won't allow us to walk away. We wait at the construction site of our dreams, but everything appears dark and desolate. The promise is not yet ready.

And what God keeps reminding me is that the bigger the promise, the more effort and time it will take to build it. God does not build dreams haphazardly, and He wants to build them to last many lifetimes. If His promise to us seems to tarry, we must come to a conclusion that the promise is bigger than we had initially expected. God will build the dream as large and strong as we are willing to wait. The only choice we have then is to cling onto hope as hard and as long as we possibly can. We can't let anything lure us away from the construction site of our dream. If God has given us His YES, we know His promise will come to pass. One day we will step foot into our Promised Land!

So instead of losing hope, we can ask God to give us a divine vision of His promises for our life. We can be in awe of all that He's already accomplished in and through us and not be discouraged by how far we still have to go. The longer we wait, the sweeter the homecoming will be. We also must be careful not to get sidetracked by other lesser dreams. We might be able to move into these dreams more quickly, but they will only accomplish a fraction of what God can accomplish if we wait on Him. Nothing will ever be more delightful than the plans that God has for us.

Wait on Him. Don't give up. Stay the course. God will turn on the lights of your dream and welcome you home before you know it!

"This vision is for a future time. It describes the end, and it will be fulfilled. If it seems slow in coming, wait patiently, for it will surely take place. It will not be delayed" (Habakkuk 2.3 NLT).

Faith Words from the Holy Land

Gratitude

Before I left for Israel, my specific prayer to God was to know the person of Jesus more. God is my Father, and the Holy Spirit is my constant companion. I know that Jesus died for my sins, but I desired to know Him like the disciples knew Him, especially witnessing the humiliation of His dying on the cross and the glory of His resurrection.

While in Jerusalem, we went to the Church of St. Peter in Gallicantu where it is thought to be the location of Caiaphas's house, the High Priest who demanded that Jesus be crucified. Down in the cellar of the house is where many believe Jesus was questioned and beaten in one of the guardrooms. Our small group gathered in that dark cell, while our guide read from Mark 14.60-65 (NLT):

"Then the high priest stood up before the others and asked Jesus, 'Well, aren't you going to answer these charges? What do you have to say for yourself?' But Jesus was silent and made no reply. Then the high priest asked him, 'Are you the Messiah, the Son of the Blessed One?'"

"Jesus said, 'I am. And you will see the Son of Man seated in the place of power at God's right hand and coming on the clouds of heaven.'"

"Then the high priest tore his clothing to show his horror and said, 'Why do we need other witnesses? You have all heard his blasphemy. What is your verdict?'"

"'Guilty!' they all cried. 'He deserves to die!'"

"Then some of them began to spit at him, and they blindfolded him and beat him with their fists. 'Prophesy to us,' they jeered. And the guards slapped him as they took him away."

Something in me shook when the words of this passage were whispered in the stony cell. Tears fell from my eyes and I began to weep uncontrollably. "Guilty!" they cried, but Jesus was sinless. It was my guilt that rang out, and it was I who deserved to die.

Then they slapped Jesus, spit on Him and took Him away. Away in my pain, away in my guilt, away in my separation from God. And Jesus cried out,"*Eli, Eli, lema sabachthani?*" which means "My God, my God, why have you abandoned me?" (Matthew 27.46 NLT).

Down there in that 2,000-year-old cellar, I met Jesus. He showed me the humiliation of our sins that He transformed into His glory. Though one man caused the corruption of sin to enter this world, Jesus has transformed our sin into His grace that is powerful to redeem us all. Gratitude for the person of Jesus filled me to overflowing, and I now walk this earth knowing that because of Jesus I will never be abandoned by God.

"And the result of God's gracious gift is very different from the result of that one man's sin. For Adam's sin led to condemnation, but God's free gift leads to our being made right with God, even though we are guilty of many sins" (Romans 5.16 NLT).

Excavation

Our tour guide took us to an excavation site in the middle of busy downtown Jerusalem. Before the dig began, this bustling area was used as a bus station for the city's transportation system. They had to actually move the entire bus depot to a new location, and I found it weird that archeologists and volunteers could be found digging in a gaping, gigantic hole with traffic careening all around.

Layers of history from the First Temple Period all the way to the Ottoman Empire lay exposed, while growth and activity progressed on all four sides of the enclosed site. Like a weeping wound on an otherwise healthy body, the excavation created an awkward yet beautiful pause in the progression of life.

The Holy Spirit whispered a profound truth to me as I walked away from the buckets of labeled dirt: "As you grow in maturity in Me, I will always have an area of excavation in your life."

Self-examination may be one of the most ignored processes of a Christian's walk of faith. We are so busy trying to progress in our spiritual maturity that we forget that God wants to excavate certain hidden areas of our hearts. We are not to live in the excavation, but we must be willing to visit it and learn from the various aspects that create our personalities, designs and habits.

There is a history in all our lives that affects our beliefs and our behaviors. In order to adjust our thinking to the God-centered standard created by Jesus, we must take time to dig through our past, so our future will not be dictated by tainted habits and thought patterns. Moreover, though the time of self-awareness may seem inconvenient, the wealth of information gained will be invaluable to learning who we are in Christ and how we fit into His Divine Kingdom Plan.

"Search me, God, and know my heart; test me and know my anxious thoughts. See if there is any offensive way in me, and lead me in the way everlasting" (Psalm 139.23-24 NIV).

Saved by Fiction

Although I write mostly nonfiction on my blog (besides my fiction meditation posts), my heart is wrapped up in the storytelling found in fiction. I didn't read a lot growing up, but during the few books I could force myself to consume, my mind would open up to the magical world of the imagination. It wasn't until my twenties that I learned to sit still long enough to cultivate the discipline of reading.

Now I read a lot. I have books everywhere. And I find myself drawn more and more to the world of my own stories. I love the complexity of human nature and how each of my story's characters is so beautifully labyrinthine. Most of all, I find that the Good News of the Gospel can be unobtrusively displayed in fiction. The core desire of all my writings is to present the love of Jesus to a desperately lost and empty world.

Through Christian Fiction, the reader is given a front-row seat to the Holy Spirit's movement in the messy lives of the characters. What a safe way to see the Gospel in action! Reading may not be for everyone but finding the Holy Spirit right in the center of a book can be transforming for many people!

For instance, our guide during my tour of the Holy Land was a Messianic Jew. Though his coming to Jesus was definitely a long process, the thing that really prompted his heart to open to the possibility of Jesus was a Christian Fiction book that a loving person gave him. Wow! When he told me this, my heart just swelled with affirmation because that's exactly what I want for my fiction books.

The years of desert writing alone, trying to wrestle out in words what the Holy Spirit wanted me to convey would seem like a moment if only one person would have an encounter with Jesus through my efforts. The hours of rewrites, the piles of rejections, the dozens of naysayers mean nothing if one lost soul would find his or her way home to God's forgiveness and grace in my words.

Time is so short, and God's children need to know that they are not alone and that there is a Creator who loves them. God designed each of us uniquely to be the light to a dark world. I want to write for God's glory because that is the passion God has placed in my heart. And I know for certain that Christian Fiction is one of many lamps that can light the way to Jesus. Jesus spoke in fiction (parables), so I know He would be pleased with my stories.

"Jesus spoke all these things to the crowd in parables; he did not say anything to them without using a parable" (Matthew 13.34 NIV).

Dead Sea

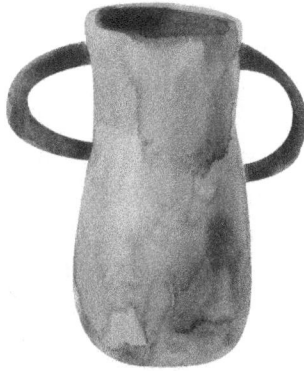

The area around the Dead Sea looks much like the desert planet Tatooine from *Star Wars*. The atmosphere surrounding the lake creates a yellow haze, and the hot sun shimmers off the salt-dusted sand. An obvious void of life encircles the briny, thick water for miles. Not only is the Dead Sea one of the "deadest" places on earth, it is also the deepest at 1,300 feet below sea level.

The "dead" and the "deep" attributes of the Dead Sea really struck a chord with me on my trip to the Holy Land. Ezekiel chapter 47 describes a symbolic rebirth of the Dead Sea. The Living Water of Jesus flows from the Temple and brings life to everything it washes over, including the Dead Sea.

"These waters go out toward the east country and down into the Arabah, then flow into the Dead sea. When they flow into the sea, the waters there become clean again. Every living thing that gathers where the river goes will live. There will be very many fish, because these waters go there and make the saltwater clean. So everything will live where the river goes. Fishermen will stand beside it. They will have places to spread their nets from Engedi to Eneglaim. The fish will be of many kinds, like the fish of the Great Sea. But its wet places and pools will not be good for animal life. They will be left for salt. All kinds of fruit trees will grow on both sides of the river. Their leaves will not dry up, and they will never stop giving fruit. They will give fruit every month because their water flows from the holy place. Their fruit will be for food and their leaves for healing" (Ezekiel 47.8-12 NLV).

The Dead Sea receives water from the "holy place" and suddenly the waters become clean and the fish and the fruit trees are numerous. Jesus specializes in bringing dead things back to life. I know he has done that in my own life. I was dead to the eternal things of God until I found Jesus.

But I also have learned that God will PURPOSELY create an area of lack or "deadness" in each of our lives, especially in the area of the promises that He has given us. Abraham, David and Joseph all had great areas of lack and need in the places God had given them promises. By faith they clung onto the hope of their God-given promises, and God showed up in mighty and miraculous ways!

God must make the lack "deep," so when He brings life to what is dead, He can fill it up with an ABUNDANCE of His Living Water! No wonder the Dead Sea is also the deepest place on earth! The larger cavity of deadness will demonstrate a greater display of God's glory! The emptier we are of our strength, abilities and resources, the more we can trust that God will provide His miraculous power and authority over our situations (2 Corinthians 12.9).

God purposely leads us into large areas of need so our obedience will bring us to a place of deep deadness, causing us to trust that God will fill the hollowness He has hewn with His abundance. We can cling onto His faithfulness and be sure that He will fulfill His promises even when they seem dead and buried. The deeper and the deader our promises seem means that God is about to do something supernatural in our lives if we don't lose hope and keep the faith!

"Abraham did not doubt God's promise. His faith in God was strong,

206

and he gave thanks to God. He was sure God was able to do what He had promised" (Romans 4.20-21 NLV).

Wilderness of Destiny

We visited the Judean Wilderness where David hid from King Saul for many years accompanied by his growing army. The desert is bordered by the Mountains of Judea to the west and the Dead Sea to the east, so the area is dry, occupying mainly rocky cliffs and caves.

I pondered how David could survive in this arid land with a band of men and their families. I looked onto the jagged landscape and watched as David's Spring trickled down the mountainous crevices. "Okay," I thought. "They have a little water. But how did they all survive so many years in this desert to become one of the strongest and most amazing militaries in all of history?"

"The wilderness prepared them," the Holy Spirit whispered.

Throughout the Bible, the wilderness plays a key role in shaping a person for his/her destiny. Abraham was called into the wilderness before he had his son (becoming the father of many nations). Joseph was called into the wilderness (slavery and prison) before he became second in command of the historically powerful nation of Egypt. The People of God were called into the wilderness before they entered their Promised Land. John the Baptist and Jesus were both called into the wilderness before they ushered in the new Era of Grace.

208

There is something about the wilderness that prepares us for all the greatness that God has in store for us. If David would have skipped his time in the wilderness, there is no doubt in my mind that he would have never been the king after God's own heart that he would eventually become. The wilderness is where he wrote many psalms, where he developed his leadership skills and, most importantly, where he learned to lean on God and obey His commands.

Many Christians want to skip the wilderness of their destiny. They want to force their God-given anointing straight into their Promised Land. However, the Promised Land is ALWAYS on the other side of the wilderness. We can't go around the wilderness; we must charge right through it.

While we wait and obey in the deserts of our promises, God is able to mold us into people after his own heart. He also prepares us for the burdens and the blessings of our destiny that could easily break or distract us. Embrace the wilderness, knowing the wealth of who you are to become will only be found in the desert places.

"A psalm of David. When he was in the Desert of Judah."

"You, God, are my God, earnestly I seek you; I thirst for you, my whole being longs for you, in a dry and parched land where there is no water" (Psalm 63.1 NIV).

Wailing Wall

The fact that I walked the city streets of Jerusalem, making my way to the Western Wall (Wailing Wall) for Shabbat (like the Christian Sabbath) still fills me with awe and gratitude. Just before sunset, the Jewish people (including many Christians) gather together at the wall, praying and crying out to God.

There is a male side and a female side of the wall, and men and women write their prayer requests on slips of paper and tuck them into the crevices of the ancient wall. Many people sing, dance, read their religious literature and lean on each other for relational support and encouragement. At the appearance of the first three stars in the sky, Shabbat is over and everyone goes home.

At the wall, rows of people wait their turn to get face to face with the layers of massive sandstone. Once their whispers of faith have been declared and their deepest confessions made, they slowly back away from the wall, bowing slightly, so the next earnest participants can take their turn.

I watched as hundreds of women—young and old—made their petitions to God, but I knew spiritually another sandstone wall stood in their way. We are a fallen creation and our sin has separated us from our perfect God (Romans 3.23). God dwells in a holy place (heaven) and even the best example of a human life would spoil it. One sin would be like scarlet ink dripping into a bucket of white paint, causing our promised eternity with the absence of sin to be tainted (Revelation 21.27).

But God loves us and He knew we would fall short of His perfect standard, so He sent Himself into this world, taking on flesh in the man of Jesus, and dying for our sins (John 3.16). He swallowed up all of our darkness, supernaturally making us white as snow (Revelation 7.14).

Though we still sin, what Jesus did on the cross continually washes us clean (1 John 1.7). And in our righteous state through Christ, we are able to walk past the thick walls of separation into the very presence of God (Romans 5.11). Our prayers fall right at the foot of the throne in Jesus' name (Hebrews 4.16).

Overwhelmed with thankfulness for a Savior that I had taken for granted, I began to praise His name. Though the voices around me cried out to God in their sinful state, I knew that I had been made right with God through Jesus (Romans 5.1). My prayers were reaching the ears of God, not because of my own greatness and perfection, but because Jesus took my lack and gave me His "righteousness, holiness and redemption" (1 Corinthians 1.30 NIV).

I am holy. I am righteous. I am perfected. I am sanctified. I stand in the glorious image of God without the ugliness of sin because of the cross, because of the empty tomb and because of the resurrected Savior. Thank You, Jesus, for rescuing me from the darkness and bringing me into Your light (Colossians 1.13). I won't allow my mistakes and flaws to prevent me from taking hold of the righteousness that is mine by faith. I won't underestimate the work You finished on the cross (John 19.30).

"But your iniquities have separated you from your God; your sins have hidden his face from you, so that he will not hear" (Isaiah 59.2 NIV).

"God made him who had no sin to be sin for us, so that in him we might become the righteousness of God" (2 Corinthians 5.21 NIV).

Skull Hill—Golgatha

Right inside the busy city of Jerusalem (just outside the ancient city walls) is where many people believe the crucifixion and burial of Jesus took place. One of the most difficult adjustments I had to make in my thinking was how close in proximity the biblical events occurred. So much happened in one little portion of this world. The death and resurrection of Jesus was such a monumental event, and it was hard to comprehend that it was just down the street from a bus stop, market and office building.

The other preconceived notion that I had to shake was how physically undramatic many locations looked compared to their spiritual relevancy. Though the beauty of Israel was stunning, the jump to the supernatural beauty I experienced when reading the Bible accounts could not be rectified. The weight of the world's sins was held on a cross in a seemingly inconspicuous location. Cars honked, people walked to school, shoppers carried their goods all while I stood face to face with Golgatha, the site of my Savior's death for my sins.

It wasn't big, scary or dramatic. It just happened to look like the face of a skull. Even if it wasn't the exact spot of the notorious Skull Hill, as my Scottish Christian guide advised, it would still pretty much look the same and be somewhere in the same general area.

The Mountain of Transfiguration, Mount of Beatitudes, Mount of Olives and Temple Mount (possible location of Mount Mariah where Isaac was bound) all looked amazingly average for having such a profound effect on history and the world.

When I think about the crucifixion itself, I realize that the actual process of crucifying people was a very normal circumstance in Jesus' time. Many people were crucified, and it wasn't at all romantic or unique. And I think about the location of the crucifixion. It was just outside the city walls (Hebrews 13.12), close to the city itself (John 19.20) and on a well-traveled road for all to see (Matthew 27.39). Crucifixions were a normal daily circumstance in Jesus' time.

But then I think of our Jesus. He didn't stand out in His appearance, and He was a simple carpenter (Matthew 13.55). He wasn't a priest or a prophet ordained by human authority and ranks, yet He was the Savior of the world. And so many people couldn't see His divinity because their eyes were limited to the natural world, oblivious to the beauty located in the supernatural realm. In fact, many people were offended by Jesus' striking normality (Mark 6.3).

> "He grew up before him like a tender shoot,
> and like a root out of dry ground.
> He had no beauty or majesty to attract us to him,
> nothing in his appearance that we should desire him.
> He was despised and rejected by mankind,
> a man of suffering, and familiar with pain.
> Like one from whom people hide their faces
> he was despised, and we held him in low esteem."
> -   Isaiah 53.2-3 (NIV)

I'm reminded through this experience that I can't always trust my physical eyes to see the glorious movement of the Holy Spirit. In reality, many of the mundane sacrifices and steps of obedience we take every day are spiritually breathtaking to God, though to us they seem boring, or worse, irrelevant. If we are being obedient to the prompting

214

of the Holy Spirit, it doesn't matter how insignificant our actions seem to the world. We must trust that God is creating something amazing in our walk of faith that would cause a band of angels to stop and take notice.

The world saw an average Man die on a plain cross that stood on a simple hill, and many people totally missed the salvation of God. As Christian, we can look past the humble and the seemingly average into the awe-inspiring glory of God.

"Therefore we are always confident and know that as long as we are at home in the body we are away from the Lord. For we live by faith, not by sight. We are confident, I say, and would prefer to be away from the body and at home with the Lord. So we make it our goal to please him, whether we are at home in the body or away from it" (2 Corinthians 5.6-9 NIV).

Take Off Your Shoes

We got to know the people on our flight to Israel very well. What started with bad weather cumulated to switched crewmembers, not enough fuel, engine problems and crew rest requirements. We were delayed a full 24 hours with the same people. In one instance, we had to leave our plane, walk across the airport, go through screening all over again, only to wait on the runway in a different plane.

I sat in a middle seat with my husband to the right of me and a young Jewish man to the left of me. Since we were heading to Israel, there were many men clad with yamakas all around us. Although the situation was tense, there seemed to be a camaraderie among the passengers, and we learned much about our companions on the plane.

By the time the flight attendant announced that they were trying to quickly get another pilot over to us before the flight time limitations hit (which caused us to lose our entire crew previously), I shrugged my shoulders and kicked off my shoes. I had been wearing the same outfit for two days; and after wrestling through a night on the airport floor in them, I felt hot, unkempt and slightly irritable.

My Jewish friend to the left of me saw that I had taken of my shoes to let my socks breathe, and he instantly pulled his shoes off. I had to smile to myself. Formality and pretense go to the wind when you're stuck. And I believe God many times allows us to stay stuck in certain areas of our lives, so we can see past our formality and pretense and be honest with our true intentions.

Why are we living out our faith with passion? Why are we aggressively seeking to do good works? Is it to fill a need of self-glory or compensate for low self-worth? Are we trying to prove ourselves subconsciously to a world that has hurt us or is there a certain person to whom we need to validate ourselves? Are we trying to work our way into God's favor or is there a nagging suspicion that we aren't good enough?

God will leave us stuck until our motives are aligned with His. He will cut through all of our Christian formalities and pretenses to get to the root of why we are living for Him. Two people can appear to be living for God with completely opposing motives, but God always gets to the heart of our intentions (1 Samuel 16.7). Sometimes it takes a season of waiting for us to see it. By default we walk in selfishness; and we must daily choose to walk in the Spirit (Galatians 5.16).

As Christians, we have full favor from God because of what Jesus has done for us on the cross. There is no need to prove ourselves to anyone because we are the righteousness of God through Jesus Christ (Romans 3.22). The work of the cross greatly overshadows our flawed lives; and when we grasp onto the truth that we are holy, righteous and valuable to God, our good works will be an overflow of that knowledge, not a desperate attempt to earn it.

God will sit you still until you find complete freedom in everything Jesus has given you (John 8.31-32). He will keep you stuck until you understand that you no longer have to strive. God loves you, and He desires for you to switch the gears of your thinking. Instead of trying to earn His love through your actions, dwell in His love and allow your actions to freely express the joy you have in Him.

Take off your shoes and rest in the Lord; and when people look at you, they may kick off their shoes too.

217

"The Lord will fight for you; you need only to be still" (Exodus 14.14 NIV).

"And God is able to bless you abundantly, so that in all things at all times, having all that you need, you will abound in every good work" (2 Corinthians 9.8 NIV).

"Now to him who is able to do immeasurably more than all we ask or imagine, according to his power that is at work within us, to him be glory in the church and in Christ Jesus throughout all generations, for ever and ever! Amen" (Ephesians 3.20-21 NIV).

Hezekiah's Tunnel

I think one of the adventures I loved most in Israel was walking through Hezekiah's Tunnel under the City of David in Jerusalem. We walked deep beneath the city, and the cool rock surrounding us was a nice reprieve from the hot summer sun. The chilly water that ran along the tunnel shocked my system, but I soon became accustomed to the fluid, invigorating liquid.

I gripped the little flashlight constructed like a harp (symbolic of King David) and followed my friend in front of me, while listening to my tall husband behind me struggle through the sometimes restrictive passages. At one moment, I turned off my flashlight just to experience the utter darkness engulfing me. I loved it. The feeling of being absolutely vulnerable to God was so exhilarating.

There are so many symbolic features that I gained from my walk under the city, but what has stayed with me most is how freeing complete reliance on God can be. When we use our eyes and our own understanding, we may tend to grope to achieve, fix or create things in our self-efforts. We wear ourselves out to accomplish very little in our limited human strength.

I know I've personally done this for so many years: trying to achieve

God's promises for me only to fail every time—always exhausted, unworthy and unable. It wasn't until God stripped me of everything that I could possibly use to achieve my dreams that I finally began to rest in Him. I experienced so much joy and peace when I found myself in the complete darkness of faith.

As I walk in obedience within His rest, I realize that my relationship with Jesus is my dream come true. All along, my promise was the Tree of Life, and the things I was striving so hard to gain were merely fruit found in Him. Submission to God may sound weak, but in actuality, it gives us His supernatural strength. I had to struggle through the slow process of dying to self to understand that I have full, abundant and purposeful life in Christ!

God created us so we can have sweet fellowship with Him. We all have an innate desire to know Him and to enjoy His presence. Sometimes, though, we have to stand still in the darkness to block out all the distractions. God will take those distractions away bit by bit because He loves us. He desires to give us a future and a hope, and He knows that only He has the ability to achieve our best life in us. The most freeing thing we can do is let go of our control and rely solely on God's sovereignty in our lives.

"Hope deferred makes the heart sick, but a dream fulfilled is a tree of life" (Proverbs 13.12 NLT).

"For I know the plans I have for you, declares the Lord, plans for welfare and not for evil, to give you a future and a hope" (Jeremiah 29.11 ESV).

"And we know that for those who love God all things work together for good, for those who are called according to his purpose" (Romans 8.28 ESV).

"But Jesus looked at them and said, 'With man this is impossible, but with God all things are possible'" (Matthew 19.26 ESV).

"Fear not, for I am with you; be not dismayed, for I am your God; I will strengthen you, I will help you, I will uphold you with my righteous right hand" (Isaiah 41.10 ESV).

Valley of Baca

The Holy Spirit encouraged me several years ago with the verses from Psalm 84.5-7 about the Valley of Baca. Being able to look over this valley in person will always be a treasured moment for me. I thought of all of us who are spiritually making our way through this valley, and I sent out a little prayer of thanksgiving and help for each of our unique journeys.

"How happy is the man whose strength is in You and in whose heart are the roads to Zion! As they pass through the dry valley of Baca, they make it a place of good water. The early rain fills the pools with good also. They go from strength to strength. Every one of them stands before God in Zion" (Psalm 84.5-7 NLV).

Baca is the Hebrew word for "weeping." Our journey as Christians will always run through this Valley of Weeping because it is only in the wilderness that we learn to die to self. Just like the unbelieving generation had to die in the wilderness before Israel could make it into their Promised Land, our flesh must die because it is what contains our lack of faith. Only our God-breathed spirits are full of faith.

The wilderness journey to my Promised Land has been very difficult for me. And as I look back, I realize I didn't quite understand the process that God was putting me through. I've struggled through many trials of faith that have strengthened my belief in God and His promises. And I've learned that our walk of faith is not about following the right formula; it's about following Jesus and getting to know Him.

In retrospect, though, I should have consumed more Living Water while I journeyed through the Valley of Baca. God had His spring of "Good Water" available to me at any time. However, I fear that I was too focused on ending the wilderness journey instead of making myself open to how God was transforming me.

I could have drunk more deeply from the Lord and found my strength renewed over and over again, yet I teetered on becoming bitter and disillusioned instead. I allowed God to quench my thirst just enough to prevent me from giving up, but I cannot attest to having a constant stream of abundant strength, faith and resolve.

What would I tell others who are walking through the Valley of Baca? I would tell them not to rush. Their speed does not change God's timing. There is a process of dying to self and it does not happen overnight. God must peel away our flesh bit by bit, lest His flash of glory cause us to fall over dead to our promises. The Valley of Baca may have its moments of pain, but joy does come in the morning (Psalm 30.5). We are all eager to get to our Zion (Promise Land), but we need to understand that Zion is already in us.

The Holy Spirit and every amazing attribute of our Father God is living in us because of what Jesus did on the cross. We have overflowing love, joy, peace, hope, patience, goodness, etc. already dwelling within our spirits (Galatians 5.22-23). Yes, God has tangible promises for each of us, but those are mere overflows of His glory and His will. Jesus' sacrifice on the cross is the ultimate gift! Even in our sinful, imperfect state, we can commune with a Holy God and receive His eternal goodness every day!

Once we learn to die to self and submit our flesh to the spirit, God will cause rivers to flow in the desert (Isaiah 43.19). He will make a way

223

where there is no way (Luke 18.27). But we can't reach the supernatural power of God until we give up on our natural strength. We have to exhaust our own strength, resources and knowledge until we finally rely on the almighty power of God. We must truly believe in the faithfulness of God. If God gives us a promise, even in the most desolate of situations, we have to remain firm in our belief!

"For no matter how many promises God has made, they are 'Yes' in Christ. And so through him the "Amen" is spoken by us to the glory of God" (2 Corinthians 1.20 NIV).

I pray you enjoyed this collection of meditations. I would be honored if you would write a review on Amazon. You can find my other fiction and non-fiction books at Amazon or on my blog, www.alisahopewagner.com.

www.ingramcontent.com/pod-product-compliance
Lightning Source LLC
LaVergne TN
LVHW051229080426
835513LV00016B/1484